tapas and other Spanish plates to share

tapas and other Spanish plates to share

RYLAND PETERS & SMALL
LONDON • NEW YORK

Senior Designer Toni Kay

Editor Delphine Lawrance

Production Controller Sarah
Kulasek-Boyd

Art Director Leslie Harrington

Editorial Director Julia Charles

First published in the UK and the USA
in 2010 by Ryland Peters & Small.
This revised edition published in 2014.
20–21 Jockey's Fields
London WC1R 4BW

and

Ryland Peters & Small Inc.
519 Broadway, 5th Floor
New York NY10012
www.rylandpeters.com

10 9 8 7 6 5 4 3 2 1

Text © Julz Beresford, Maxine Clark, Ross
Dobson, Clare Ferguson, Jennie Shapter,
Linda Tubby and Ryland Peters & Small
2010, 2014

Design and photographs
© Ryland Peters & Small 2010, 2014

ISBN: 978-1-84975-570-2

A CIP record for this book is available from
the British Library.

Printed and bound in China

contents

introduction

The word 'tapas' stems from the Spanish verb *tapar*, meaning 'to cover'. Legend has it that the tapas tradition began when King Alfonso X of Castile recovered from an illness by drinking wine alongside small dishes in-between meals. He then made it illegal for taverns to serve wine to customers unless it was accompanied by a small snack or tapa. The word became a kind of loophole in the law to allow drinkers to consume alcohol.

Tapas have evolved in Spain by incorporating ingredients and influences from several different countries. The invasion of the North African Moors in the 8th century brought almonds, citrus fruits and fragrant spices. The influence of their presence remains today, especially in Andalusia. The discovery of the New World brought tomatoes, sweet and chilli peppers, corn, beans and potatoes. These were easy to grow thanks to Spain's temperate climate.

Tapas now enjoy worldwide appeal as they are a highly sociable way to eat, making them the perfect choice for sharing. The mouth-watering recipes included in this book are designed to be combined and many can be made ahead. Nearly all of the required ingredients are easily sourced, but should you have any difficulties, turn to the handy directory of suppliers on page 142. Mix and match the dishes as you please to create a meat-, seafood- or vegetable-orientated menu.

meat and poultry

chicken with garlic
pollo al ajillo

This flavoursome dish finds its way onto almost every tapas menu in Spain and varies only slightly. It's so common, yet so simple to make. If you're unable to get hold of Brandy de Jerez, substitute it for Cognac or Armagnac.

8 chicken wings

1 teaspoon oak-smoked sweet Spanish paprika

1 tablespoon lemon juice

2 tablespoons olive oil

6 garlic cloves, coarsely crushed

150 ml/^{2}/$_3$ cup Brandy de Jerez

sea salt and freshly ground black pepper

SERVES 4

Put the chicken wings in a non-reactive bowl, then rub the paprika evenly over the skin. Add the lemon juice, cover and let marinate in the refrigerator for 2 hours.

Heat the oil in a heavy-based frying pan/skillet until smoking, add the chicken and brown on all sides. Reduce the heat, add the garlic and cook for a further 2 minutes. Add the brandy, tilt the pan/skillet to catch the flame and burn off the alcohol until the flames subside. Cover with a lid and simmer for 10 minutes. Add salt and pepper to taste, then serve.

catalan chickpea salad
ensalada catalana de garbanzos

This delicious, warm salad relies on just a handful of ingredients. With such a wonderful combination of flavours, you would never guess that it has a cooking time of just five minutes. You can forgo the pine nuts, but they do add a lovely bite to this salad.

3 tablespoons extra virgin olive oil

1 red onion, sliced

2 garlic cloves, chopped

200 g/8 oz. chorizo, sliced

2 bay leaves, bruised

2 tablespoons pine nuts, toasted in a dry frying pan/skillet (optional)

400 g/2 cups canned chickpeas, drained, reserving 2 tablespoons of their liquid

coarsely ground black pepper

1 small tomato, finely chopped, to serve

SERVES 4

Heat the oil in a frying pan/skillet, add the onion, garlic, chorizo and bay leaves and sauté over gentle heat for 5 minutes or until softened but not browned. Stir in the toasted pine nuts, if using, and chickpeas with their liquid. Heat until the flavours are combined, mashing a little with a fork.

Sprinkle with pepper and the chopped tomato and serve hot, warm or cool, but never chilled.

chorizo in red wine
chorizo al vino tinto

Chorizo comes in many different varieties. You can get smoked, unsmoked, fresh
and cured. Spicy fresh chorizo, the size of regular breakfast sausages, works well in this
recipe. Large quantities of paprika give the dish a rich colour and a pungent flavour.
Each region of Spain has its own version – this one is simple and delicious.

1 tablespoon olive oil

300 g/10 oz. small, spicy fresh
chorizo sausages, cut into 1-cm/
1/2-inch slices

100 ml/1/2 cup red wine

crusty bread, to serve

SERVES 4

Put the oil in a heavy-based frying pan/skillet and heat until
smoking. Add the chorizo and cook for 1 minute. Reduce
the heat, add the wine and cook for 5 minutes. Transfer to
a serving dish and set aside to develop the flavours. Serve
warm with crusty bread.

pork and veal turnovers
empanadillas de carne

These small, savoury pies are great to serve alongside other tapas. They can be made days in advance and frozen, making them the perfect choice if you have a large group of guests to feed and you want to be free to entertain.

freshly squeezed juice of 1 lemon

100 g/1 stick butter

225 g/1¹⁄₂ cups plain/all-purpose flour

a pinch of sea salt

STUFFING

1 tablespoon olive oil

1 tablespoon finely grated onion

1 garlic clove, crushed

100 g/4 oz. minced/ground pork

100 g/4 oz. minced/ground veal

1 tablespoon tomato paste

1 tablespoon white wine

1 teaspoon dried oregano

1 teaspoon chopped fresh parsley

1 hard-boiled egg, mashed

2 eggs

sea salt and freshly ground
white pepper

oil, for frying

*a biscuit/cookie cutter, 8 cm/3 inches
diameter*

an electric deep-fryer (optional)

SERVES 4

To make the pastry, put the lemon juice, butter and 100 ml/¹⁄₂ cup water in a saucepan, heat until melted, then let cool. When cool, sift in the flour and salt and mix slowly. Knead on a floured surface until the mixture loses its stickiness. Wrap in clingfilm/plastic wrap and refrigerate for 2 hours.

Meanwhile, to make the stuffing, heat the oil in a frying pan/skillet. Add the onion, garlic, pork and veal and cook for 3 minutes. Add the tomato paste, wine, oregano and parsley, then cook for 5 minutes. Remove from the heat, season well and add the hard-boiled egg. Let cool, cover and chill.

Put the pastry on a floured surface and roll out to a 5-mm/¹⁄₈-inch thickness. Cut into 8-cm/3-inch rounds with a biscuit/cookie cutter and spoon a heaped teaspoon of the stuffing into the centre of each round. Brush the edges with water and fold in half. Using your index fingers, push the edges together to create a rippled effect.

Fill a saucepan or deep-fryer one-third full of oil or to the manufacturer's recommended level and heat to 195°C (380°F). Put the eggs in a bowl, add 2 tablespoons cold water and beat lightly. Working in batches, dip each turnover in the beaten egg mixture, deep-fry for 3 minutes until golden brown, then serve immediately.

spicy chicken empanada
empanada gallega

2 tablespoons olive oil

1 large onion, finely chopped

2 garlic cloves, crushed

500 g/1 lb. skinless chicken breast, cut into 2.5-cm/1-inch pieces

4 tablespoons/$\frac{1}{4}$ cup dry white wine

3 tomatoes, skinned and chopped, reserving any juices

125 g/4 oz. cured chorizo, cut into thick slices

about 3 tablespoons chopped fresh oregano

$\frac{1}{2}$ teaspoon hot paprika

4 roasted red piquillo peppers, from a jar, coarsely chopped

2 tablespoons chopped fresh flat leaf parsley

4 hard-boiled eggs, halved

coarse sea salt and freshly ground black pepper

PASTRY

450 g/3 cups plain/all-purpose flour

75 g/$\frac{1}{2}$ cup fine cornmeal or polenta

1 sachet fast-action dried yeast

1$\frac{1}{2}$ teaspoons fine sea salt

3 tablespoons unsalted butter

200 ml/a scant 1 cup milk

2 eggs

1 egg, beaten with 1 tablespoon water, for glazing

a baking pan with shallow sides, 32 x 22 cm/11 x 9 inches, greased

MAKES 8 SLICES

Heat the oil in a saucepan, add the onion and garlic and sauté over medium heat for 5 minutes until softened but not coloured. Increase the heat and stir in the chicken, moving it around until it turns opaque. Add the wine, the tomatoes and their juices and cook until the sauce starts to thicken and the chicken has almost cooked.

Stir in the chorizo, oregano and paprika and season. Transfer to a bowl and let the mixture cool completely.

To make the pastry, mix the flour, cornmeal, yeast and salt in a bowl. Put the butter and milk in a saucepan and heat until the butter has melted. When the milk has cooled a little, beat the 2 eggs in a bowl and add the milk.

Make a hollow in the flour and pour in the milk mixture. Mix with your hands to form a ball. Transfer to a floured work surface and knead for about 5 minutes or until smooth and elastic. Put the dough in a lightly oiled bowl, cover with clingfilm/plastic wrap and set aside in a warm place until it has almost doubled in size (about an hour).

Preheat the oven to 180°C (350°F) Gas 4.

Halve the dough and cover one piece. Roll out the other piece to the size of the baking pan, leaving a 2-cm/1-inch overhang. Press the dough into the pan. Stir the peppers and parsley into the cold filling, then spoon it evenly over the dough. Nestle the halved eggs into the filling.

Roll out the rest of the dough to fit the tin and drape over the top. Brush egg wash on the edges of the pastry. Bring the overhang up over the top pastry and crimp a little to seal. Brush with the remaining egg wash, make a few slits in the top and bake for 30 minutes until golden (if over-browning, cover with foil). Serve hot or cold, in slices.

ham and chicken croquettes
croquetas de jamón serrano

Serrano ham, a Spanish mountain ham, is one of Spain's greatest culinary creations. It is pungent, sweet and slightly salty – a key ingredient in many Spanish recipes. Mixed with creamy ingredients, it is a surprise filling for this crisp and crunchy tapas favourite.

250 ml/1 cup milk

1/2 small onion, sliced

1 bay leaf

2 black peppercorns

a sprig of fresh thyme

2 tablespoons unsalted butter

3 tablespoons plain/all-purpose flour

a pinch of oak-smoked sweet Spanish paprika

a pinch of freshly grated nutmeg

150 g/6 oz. Serrano ham, finely chopped

100 g/4 oz. cooked chicken breast, finely chopped

300 g/2 cups dried breadcrumbs

2 eggs, lightly beaten

oil, for cooking and deep-frying

an electric deep-fryer (optional)

SERVES 4

Put the milk in a saucepan, add the onion, bay leaf, pepper and thyme and heat until just below boiling point. Remove from the heat, let cool, then strain into a bowl.

Melt the butter gently in a saucepan, stir in the flour and cook for 2 minutes, stirring constantly. When the roux begins to brown, slowly add the milk, stirring to prevent lumps forming. Continue to cook, adding the paprika and nutmeg.

Heat 1 tablespoon oil in a small frying pan/skillet, add the Serrano ham and sauté until the fat starts to run. Add the Serrano ham and chicken to the white sauce and continue cooking until the sauce thickens, about 2 minutes.

Remove from the heat and let cool. Cover and refrigerate for 3 hours or overnight. Shape the mixture into croquettes about 6 x 2 cm/1 x 2 inches. Lightly roll in the breadcrumbs, dip into the beaten eggs and roll in the breadcrumbs again. Cover and chill for 1 hour or overnight.

Fill a saucepan or deep-fryer one-third full of oil or to the manufacturer's recommended level and heat to 195°C (380°F). Add the croquettes and fry, in batches if necessary, for 3 minutes or until golden brown. Serve immediately.

migas with serrano ham
migas de extremadura

Migas, meaning 'breadcrumbs' in Spanish, are a national treasure. They are simply bread sprinkled with salted water, then fried in olive oil. These are often flavoured with Serrano ham, but plain ones are served in many ways – sometimes with grapes, fried eggs or even with hot chocolate. There are countless regional variations; these are from Extremadura and they go well with Cava.

200 g/8 oz. dry 2-day-old country bread, crusts removed

125 ml/¹/₂ cup extra virgin olive oil

100 g/4 oz. Serrano ham or streaky/lean slab bacon, cut into 5-mm/¹/₄-inch pieces, or bacon lardons

3 garlic cloves, bruised with the back of a knife

1 fat dried red chilli, such as ñora or ancho, deseeded and finely chopped

coarse sea salt

SERVES 4

Cut the bread into fingers, spread it out on a kitchen towel, then sprinkle lightly with water and a little salt. Wrap up in the towel and leave for 2 hours. Unwrap and break the bread into big pieces.

Heat 2 teaspoons of the oil in a frying pan/skillet, add the ham and fry until crisp. Drain on paper towels.

Wipe the pan clean and heat the remaining oil. Add the garlic, sauté until golden, then remove and discard. Add all the breadcrumbs at once and stir-fry until evenly golden. Stir in the chilli and Serrano ham and serve very hot. Eat with your fingers or using a small spoon.

lamb with lemon
cordero al limón

This recipe is a favourite in Aragón and Murcia in central Spain, where meat-based tapas are popular. The use of pineapple for tenderizing meat is a technique found in South-east Asia. It perhaps arrived in Spain from the former Spanish colony of the Philippines. Serve this dish with a good Rioja.

250 g/8 oz. lean lamb, such as the neck or loin

225 g/8 oz. canned pineapple slices, drained

10 cloves

1 lemon, halved

5 garlic cloves, peeled

2 tablespoons olive oil

a sprig of fresh rosemary

½ small onion, finely chopped

a pinch of oak-smoked sweet Spanish paprika

SERVES 4

Cut the lamb into 2-cm/¾-inch cubes. Put them in a bowl, cover with the pineapple slices and let marinate overnight, covered, in the refrigerator.

Preheat the oven to 150°C (300°F) Gas 2.

Stick the cloves into the lemon and put it in a roasting dish. Add the garlic, oil and rosemary. Remove the pineapple from the lamb and rub in the onion and paprika. Add the lamb to the roasting dish and cook in the oven for 15 minutes. Take out of the oven, cover with foil and set aside for 10 minutes before serving.

meatballs in tomato sauce
albóndigas

Albóndigas are one of the classic tapas dishes and most deserving of their popularity. You can choose to serve these meatballs with alioli (see page 117) and lemon rather than the tomato sauce – this is a common Spanish variation. The meatballs reheat well.

150 g/6 oz. minced/ground pork

150 g/6 oz. minced/ground veal

1 teaspoon freshly squeezed lemon juice

$^1/_2$ small onion, finely chopped

2 garlic cloves, crushed

2 tablespoons chopped fresh
flat leaf parsley

$^1/_2$ teaspoon freshly grated nutmeg

$^1/_2$ teaspoon ground cloves

30 g/$^1/_4$ cup dried breadcrumbs

1 egg

1 tablespoon single/light cream

plain/all-purpose flour, for dusting

2 tablespoons olive oil

sea salt and freshly ground white pepper

TOMATO SAUCE

125 ml/$^1/_2$ cup white wine

400 g/14 oz. canned chopped tomatoes

$^1/_2$ small onion, finely chopped

2 garlic cloves, crushed

$^1/_2$ teaspoon oak-smoked sweet
Spanish paprika

1 fresh bay leaf

SERVES 4

To make the meatballs, put the pork and veal in a bowl, then add the lemon juice, onion, garlic, parsley, nutmeg, cloves, breadcrumbs, egg, cream, salt and pepper. Mix well, then roll into walnut-sized balls. Dust with flour.

Heat the oil in a flameproof casserole until smoking, add the meatballs and sauté until browned on all sides. Reduce the heat to low. Add the wine, tomatoes, onion, garlic, paprika, bay leaf and 100 ml/$^1/_3$ cup water. Cover and simmer for 1 hour. The mixture should be quite liquid, so add extra water if necessary. Serve warm.

spicy moorish kebabs
pinchitos morunos

This recipe is from Andalusia, where you see it in almost every tapas bar. The region is renowned for simple food, so this is a quick, easy recipe that leaves more time for other things, like socializing with guests.

2 tablespoons olive oil

2 garlic cloves, crushed

1 dried red chilli, crushed

1 teaspoon ground cumin

1 teaspoon ground fennel

1 teaspoon oak-smoked sweet Spanish paprika

freshly squeezed juice of 1 lemon

2 tablespoons chopped fresh flat leaf parsley

1 tablespoon dry sherry

500 g/1 lb. pork tenderloin

metal kebab skewers or bamboo, soaked in water for 30 minutes

SERVES 4

Put the oil, garlic, chilli, cumin, fennel, paprika, lemon juice, parsley and sherry in a bowl and mix well. Cut the pork into 2-cm/³⁄₄-inch cubes and add to the bowl. Cover and chill overnight in the refrigerator.

When ready to cook, preheat a grill or broiler until very hot. Thread the pork onto the skewers and grill for 10 minutes, turning often – take care not to overcook the meat. Remove from the heat and set aside for 10 minutes. Serve warm.

hot sandwiches
emparedados calientes

Serve these sandwiches on a bamboo skewer with bowls of olives and pimientos de Padrón, if you can find them in a Spanish food shop. Emparedados make a great snack served with a glass of draught beer or a good chilled Chardonnay from Penedès.

8 slices of Serrano ham

12 thin slices of cured chorizo

8 slices of 3-day-old bread, crusts removed

2 tablespoons grated Manchego cheese

4 eggs, beaten

90 ml/$\frac{1}{2}$ cup extra virgin olive oil

fine sea salt and freshly ground black pepper

TO SERVE

olives

pimientos de Padrón (optional)

bamboo skewers

SERVES 4

Divide the Serrano ham and chorizo between 4 slices of the bread, grind over some pepper and sprinkle the grated cheese on top of the chorizo, keeping it to the centre of the slices. Put the remaining slices of bread on top and press down firmly.

Put the beaten eggs, salt and pepper in a flat dish large enough to take 2 sandwiches at a time and dip the sandwiches in the mixture.

Heat half the oil in a non-stick frying pan/skillet large enough to take 2 sandwiches at a time, then sauté over medium heat until crisp and golden, 3–3$\frac{1}{2}$ minutes each side. Repeat with the remaining oil and sandwiches. Cut into triangles, thread onto bamboo skewers and serve while hot with olives and pimientos de Padrón, if using.

Note Pimientos de Padrón are tiny green peppers named after Padrón in Galicia – available in specialist food shops. Simply sautéed in olive oil, then sprinkled with salt, you eat them off the stalk, leaving the seeds behind. Be warned – about one in six will be as hot as a chilli!

To make them, heat 2 tablespoons olive oil in a large frying pan/skillet. Working in batches, add 200 g/8 oz. fresh green pimientos de Padrón and sauté, shaking the pan/skillet, until the skins blister and the green colour intensifies. Remove from the pan, pile onto a plate and sprinkle with salt.

fish and seafood

marinated anchovies
boquerones en vinagre

People tend to be intimidated by these little fish, but have no fear, they are easy to prepare and taste simply divine. Soon, you will be using these little gems with everything. They are popular all over Spain.

150 g/6 oz. fresh anchovies*

100 ml/scant $\frac{1}{2}$ cup good-quality white wine vinegar

3 garlic cloves, sliced

1 tablespoon chopped fresh flat leaf parsley

100 ml/scant $\frac{1}{2}$ cup olive oil

SERVES 4

*If fresh anchovies are unavailable, use any small fish you can find. Aim for 6–8 cm/2–3 inches long.

To clean the anchovies, run your finger down the belly side and open up the fish. Pull the spine from the head and separate it from the flesh. Remove the head. Wash the fish and let dry on paper towels.

Put the anchovies in a plastic container and pour in the vinegar. Cover and let marinate in the refrigerator overnight. Rinse the anchovies and put in a serving dish with the garlic, parsley and oil, cover and chill overnight. Return to room temperature. You can keep the anchovies in the refrigerator to eat another day – they only get better with time.

marinated octopus
pulpo a la vinagreta

Some people avoid cooking octopus because they think they can be tough. In Spain, octopus are banged against the jetty by the fishermen to make them tender. If you don't have a fisherman on hand, tap the octopus with a meat mallet or buy them frozen (freezing also helps tenderize them). Then you should cook them long and slow at a low temperature. Octopus keeps well and the longer you marinate it, the better the flavour.

about 500 g/12 oz. small octopus tentacles

3 tablespoons olive oil

2 tablespoons red wine vinegar

2 garlic cloves, crushed

3 tablespoons chopped fresh flat leaf parsley

$\frac{1}{2}$ teaspoon oak-smoked sweet Spanish paprika

$\frac{1}{2}$ teaspoon dried chilli/hot red pepper flakes

1 tablespoon capers, chopped

freshly squeezed juice of 1 lemon

sea salt and freshly ground black pepper

SERVES 4

If the octopus hasn't been frozen or tenderized by the fisherman, you should throw it against a hard surface 10 times or more. Put it on a chopping board, cut off the head just below the eyes and discard, then squeeze out and discard the beak, which is in the centre of the tentacles. Rinse out the bodies.

Bring a large saucepan of water to the boil, then blanch the octopus for 30 seconds at a time, repeating 4–5 times. Return the octopus to the saucepan, cover with a lid and simmer for 1 hour.

Test the octopus for tenderness – if it's still tough, continue cooking for another 20 minutes. Remove from the heat, let cool, then drain. Cut the tentacles into 2-cm/1-inch lengths and the bodies into bite-sized pieces.

Heat the oil in a frying pan/skillet, add the vinegar, garlic, 2 tablespoons of the parsley, paprika, chilli flakes, capers and octopus. Bring to the boil, then simmer for 3 minutes. Transfer to a plastic or ceramic dish and let cool. Season, then cover and let marinate in the refrigerator overnight.

Serve at room temperature with the lemon juice and the remaining parsley.

marinated sardines
sardinas en escabeche

Escabeche, which means 'pickle', is a very old method of preserving food, especially fish. The pickle effectively 'cooks' the flesh in lemon juice or vinegar. This one is in vinegar, which is perfect with the healthy, sweet oiliness of sardines. Don't be put off by cleaning the fish – it's easy and as soon as you get the hang of these little ones you'll be cleaning bigger fish in no time.

8 fresh sardines, about 500 g/1 lb.

2 tablespoons olive oil

50 ml/scant $\frac{1}{2}$ cup good-quality white wine vinegar

100 ml/scant $\frac{1}{2}$ cup dry white wine

2 garlic cloves, sliced

4 fresh bay leaves

1 teaspoon fennel seeds, lightly crushed

$\frac{1}{2}$ teaspoon dried chilli/hot red pepper flakes

2 sprigs of fresh thyme

4 slices of lemon

crusty bread, to serve

SERVES 4

To clean the sardines, wash them in cold water and scrape off any scales. Put the fish on a board, take off the head, run a knife from the head halfway down the belly side and scrape out the insides. Wash the fish and let dry on a kitchen towel. Run your thumb down the inside of the fish along the bone and squash the fillets flat. Gently pull the backbone away from the flesh towards the tail. Cut with scissors.

Heat the oil in a heavy-based frying pan/skillet, add the vinegar, wine, garlic, bay leaves, fennel, chilli/pepper flakes and thyme, then bring to the boil for 3 minutes. Add the sardines skin side up, then remove from the heat.

Arrange the sardines in a single layer in a plastic or ceramic dish, put the slices of lemon on top, then pour over the liquid and cover with clingfilm/plastic wrap. Let marinate in the refrigerator overnight. Serve at room temperature with crusty bread. You can return them to the refrigerator to eat another day – they only get better with time.

spanish marinated tuna
bonito marinado

Barcelona, Seville and Madrid buzz with culinary finesse, and today's young chefs often incorporate outside influences, with great skill, into classic dishes. Although raw tuna with soy sauce in its marinade seems more like a Japanese idea than a Spanish one, it is a well-loved, new-style seafood tapas dish. Select a neat rectangle of top-quality belly tuna, at least 2-cm/1-inch thick, and skinless, boneless and well trimmed of all cartilage.

200 g/8 oz. very fresh belly tuna, such as loin of yellowfin, cut into 1-cm/^{1}/$_2$-inch chunks

1 tablespoon light soy sauce

1 tablespoon sherry vinegar

1 teaspoon toasted sesame oil

1 tablespoon extra virgin olive oil

1 garlic clove, crushed

1 tablespoon toasted sesame seeds (optional)

1 tablespoon blue poppy seeds (optional)

crisp salad leaves or herbs (optional)

SERVES 4

Put the tuna, soy sauce, vinegar, sesame oil, olive oil and garlic in a bowl and stir well. Cover and let marinate in the refrigerator for 5 minutes or up to 2 hours.

Drain, reserving the marinade, then arrange the chunks of tuna in rows on small serving dishes. Add lines of the sesame and poppy seeds, if using, then sprinkle with the marinade or leave plain. Add a few salad leaves or herbs, if using. Serve the remaining marinade on the side.

seafood zarzuela
zarzuela de mariscos

250 ml/1 cup dry white wine

12 fresh mussels, scrubbed and debearded

12 fresh clams, scrubbed and rinsed

250 g/8 oz. each of monkfish and halibut fillet, skinned and cut into large chunks

6 large uncooked peeled prawns/shrimp

5 tablespoons/$^1/_3$ cup virgin olive oil

6 cooked langoustines or extra prawns/shrimp

sea salt and freshly ground black pepper

2 lemons, cut into wedges, to serve

PICADA (Catalan bread & nut paste)

2 slices of fried white bread, in cubes

2 garlic cloves, coarsely chopped

9 almonds, coarsely chopped

125 ml/$^1/_2$ cup extra virgin olive oil

SOFREGIT (Catalan tomato sauce)

2 tablespoons olive oil

1 onion, finely chopped

1 garlic clove, crushed

2 teaspoons oak-smoked sweet paprika

200 g/8 oz. canned chopped tomatoes

$^1/_2$ teaspoon saffron threads, soaked

3 bay leaves

sea salt and freshly ground black pepper

SERVES 4

To make the picada, put the fried bread in a small processor with the garlic and almonds and blend finely. With the motor running, gradually add the oil to form a loose paste.

To prepare the mussels and clams, put the wine in a large saucepan and bring to the boil. Add the mussels and clams, cover and cook over medium heat for about 2 minutes – shake the pan after 1 minute – until all the shells have opened. Discard any that haven't. Pour into a colander set over a bowl to catch all the liquid. Transfer the mussels and clams to a bowl and cover loosely. Reserve the liquid to use in the sofregit.

To make the sofregit, heat the oil in a saucepan, add the onion and garlic and sauté gently until pale golden and soft. Stir in the paprika, tomatoes and saffron and its soaking water. Pour the mussel liquid carefully through a fine-meshed sieve, leaving any sediment behind. Add the bay leaves, salt and pepper. Cover and cook over medium heat for 10 minutes. Add a little water if the mixture gets too thick.

Season the monkfish, halibut and prawns/shrimp with salt and pepper. Heat 2 tablespoons of the oil in a frying pan/skillet, add the pieces of monkfish and halibut and sauté until lightly golden on both sides. Remove to a plate and keep them warm. Deglaze the pan/skillet with 3 tablespoons water and pour into the simmering sofregit.

Wipe the frying pan/skillet, add the remaining 3 tablespoons oil along with the prawns/shrimp and sauté just until they turn pink on both sides. Add the langoustines to heat through for 1 minute, turning frequently. Pour in the cooked sofregit and add the rest of the seafood, including the mussels and clams. Heat very gently for a few minutes to ensure everything is cooked through. Loosen the picada with a little liquid from the pan and mix into the seafood. Serve with the lemon wedges.

clams in tomato and saffron sauce
almejas a la marinera

Spain has the longest coastline in Europe. Therefore, seafood forms a major part of the Spanish diet. Almejas (clams) are popular, especially in Catalonia. They are easy to cook and always delicious. You can simply steam them in white wine or sherry. However, the sweetness of the tomatoes and saffron in this recipe is especially delicious.

500 g/1 lb. small fresh clams

a pinch of saffron threads

1 tablespoon olive oil

$\frac{1}{2}$ small onion, finely chopped

2 garlic cloves, crushed

75 ml/$\frac{1}{3}$ cup dry sherry

2 tablespoons tomato paste

1 tablespoon chopped fresh flat leaf parsley

a pinch of oak-smoked sweet Spanish paprika

a pinch of cayenne pepper

1 tablespoon ground/slivered almonds

crusty bread, to serve

SERVES 4

To clean the clams, put them in a bowl of cold salty water and let soak for 2 hours. This should help get rid of some of the grit. Put the saffron in a bowl with 1 tablespoon hot water and let soak.

Heat the oil in a saucepan over gentle heat, then add the onion and cook for 3 minutes. Add the garlic, sherry, tomato paste, parsley, paprika, cayenne pepper, saffron with its soaking water and 50 ml/$\frac{1}{4}$ cup water. Bring to the boil and let boil for 4 minutes.

Add the clams, cover with a lid and cook for 4 minutes until the shells steam open (discard any that don't). Stir in the almonds and cook for 1 further minute. Remove the saucepan from the heat and set aside, covered with a lid, for 5 minutes. Serve warm with bread.

44

spanish clams with serrano ham
almejas con jamón serrano

Mediterranean live clams usually go straight into the cooking pot, with oil and garlic. However, because Spanish cured hams are so exceptional, adding even a little will season and enliven many such savoury dishes. *Mar i montaña* (sea and mountains) – the combining of meat with fish or seafood is a typically Catalan cooking idea. The cooking time for this recipe is just a few minutes, meaning that this tapas dish is ready in a flash.

2 tablespoons extra virgin olive oil

500 g/1 lb. small fresh clams, or frozen uncooked clams

50 g/2 oz. Serrano ham, cut into thin strips

1 small green chilli, deseeded and chopped

2 garlic cloves, sliced

4 tablespoons/¼ cup white wine or cider

2 tablespoons chopped spring onion/scallion tops, chives or parsley

SERVES 4

Put the oil, clams, Serrano ham, chilli and garlic in a saucepan and stir over high heat. When the Serrano ham is cooked and the clams begin to open, add the wine, cover the saucepan and shake it to mix the ingredients. Cook on high for a further 2–3 minutes or until the clams have opened and are cooked (discard any that don't open).

Sprinkle with the chopped spring onion/scallion tops. Cover again for 1 minute, then ladle into shallow soup bowls.

white beans with clams
alubias blancas con almejas

250 g/1¼ cups alubias (Spanish dried white beans), or dried white haricot or cannellini beans, soaked for 8–10 hours or overnight

1 onion, halved

3 garlic cloves, peeled

1 carrot, halved

1 fresh bay leaf

a sprig of fresh flat leaf parsley

a small pinch of saffron threads, soaked in 1 tablespoon boiling water

sea salt

crusty bread, to serve

CLAMS

125 ml/½ cup dry white wine

36 small live clams

4 tablespoons olive oil

1 onion, finely chopped

2 garlic cloves, crushed

1 tablespoon oak-smoked sweet Spanish paprika

1 medium dried red chilli, deseeded and roughly ground

2 tablespoons coarsely chopped fresh flat leaf parsley

coarse sea salt and freshly ground black pepper

a medium-sized piece of muslin/cheesecloth

SERVES 4

Drain the soaked beans and put in a large saucepan with 800 ml/1 quart cold water.

Add the onion halves, garlic, carrot, bay leaf and parsley and bring slowly to the boil. When the froth threatens to boil over, splash 200 ml/1 cup cold water into the pan to 'scare' the beans. Skim off the froth, return to the boil and simmer for 10 minutes. Add another 200 ml/1 cup cold water to the pan, return to simmering point, then continue cooking for about 1 hour until tender. Remove the onion, carrot and parsley, add salt and cook for another 5 minutes. Drain over a bowl, then put the beans back in the pan with the saffron, its soaking water and 100 ml/½ cup of the bean cooking liquid. Keep the lid on until ready to use. This stage can be done in advance.

To prepare the clams, heat the wine in a saucepan until boiling, add a little salt, then add the clams. Cook, covered, for about 2 minutes until they open (discard any that don't). Drain through a colander set over a bowl and cover the colander with a plate. Rinse out the saucepan, add the oil and heat for 30 seconds. Add the onion and garlic, cover and cook over low heat for about 10 minutes without browning. Stir in the paprika, chilli and season to taste.

Remove half the clams from their shells and discard the shells. Add all the clams to the onion mixture and carefully pour the clam liquid through a muslin/cheesecloth-lined sieve into the pan, taking care to leave 1 cm/½ inch of liquid in the bottom of the bowl because this may contain some grit. Heat the mixture just enough to warm up the clams.

Heat the beans and add the clam mixture. Ladle into heated soup plates. Sprinkle with the parsley and serve with bread.

fried squid roman-style
calamares a la romana

This classic tapas dish is served just about everywhere in Spain and is ever so simple and quick to make. The batter is deliciously light. The way to make the squid tender is to buy them small and not cook them for too long.

500 g/1 lb. small squid, or 150 g/
6 oz. cleaned squid tubes

2 eggs

plain/all-purpose flour, for coating

sea salt

olive oil, for frying

1 lemon, cut into wedges, to serve

an electric deep-fryer (optional)

SERVES 4

To clean the squid, pull the head away from the body (tube). Rub your thumb down the length of the tube and lever off the wings and discard. Remove the translucent quill inside and rub the pinky skin off the outside. Wash well under cold water. Cut the tubes into 1-cm/$\frac{1}{2}$ inch slices.

Put the eggs in a bowl, add 2 tablespoons water and beat well. Put the flour on a plate and sprinkle generously with salt. Working on one at a time, dip the squid rings into the egg mixture, then into the flour, making sure they are well coated. Set aside.

Fill a saucepan or deep-fryer one-third full of oil or to the manufacturer's recommended level and heat to 195°C (380°F). Cook the squid rings in batches until golden brown. Make sure the temperature remains the same for each batch. Remove with a slotted spoon and drain on paper towels. Let rest for 5 minutes, then serve with the lemon wedges.

squid with mayonnaise
sepia con alioli

This simple dish will bring a lovely taste of seaside Spain to your table. The squid may well be deep-fried, but they taste lovely and light, with the alioli making the perfect accompaniment as a dipping sauce.

100–200 g/$^2/_3$–1$^1/_3$ cups semolina flour

$^1/_2$–1 teaspoon sea salt

$^1/_2$–1 teaspoon dried oregano or marjoram leaves, crumbled

8 medium squid or cuttlefish tubes, sliced into 1-cm/$^1/_2$-inch rounds

extra virgin olive oil, for deep-frying

TO SERVE

$^1/_2$ lemon (optional)

alioli (page 117)

an electric deep-fryer (optional)

SERVES 4

Put the semolina flour, salt and oregano in a bowl. Pat the squid rings dry with paper towels and toss them in the flour mixture until well coated.

Fill a deep frying pan/skillet or an electric deep-fryer one-third full with oil, or to the manufacturer's recommended level. Heat to 195°C (380°F) or until a 1-cm/$^1/_2$-inch cube of bread browns in about 30 seconds. Fry the prepared squid in the hot oil in batches of about 8. Cook for 30–45 seconds, the minimum time it takes to set the seafood to firm whiteness and make the coating crisp. Remove, drain and keep hot. Continue until all of the squid are cooked.

Serve a pile of squid rings on each plate, with the ½ lemon, if using, and a large spoonful of alioli.

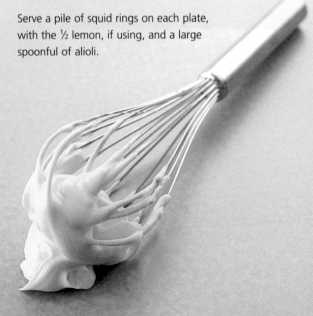

stuffed calamares
calamares rellenos

Use small squid in this recipe if you can get hold of them as they are more likely to be tender. The combination of the squid with the spicy chorizo, chilli flakes and parsley makes this dish very fresh-tasting but with a mean little kick.

5 tablespoons/¹/₃ cup extra virgin olive oil

1 medium onion, finely chopped

16 cleaned baby squid with tentacles, about 7 cm/3 inches long (see note)

50 g/2 oz. chorizo, finely chopped

¹/₂ teaspoon dried chilli flakes

70 g/¹/₂ cup pine nuts

2 garlic cloves, finely chopped

2 tablespoons chopped fresh flat leaf parsley, plus extra coarsely chopped, to serve

175 ml/³/₄ cup measured fresh breadcrumbs

TOMATO SAUCE

2 tablespoons extra virgin olive oil

1 onion, finely chopped

1 garlic clove, finely chopped

¹/₂ teaspoon sugar

6 medium tomatoes, skinned, deseeded and finely chopped, reserving any juices

wooden cocktail sticks/toothpicks

SERVES 4

Preheat the oven to 190°C (375°F) Gas 5.

Heat 3 tablespoons of the oil in a frying pan/skillet, add the onion and sauté until soft and pale golden. Add the chopped tentacles and sauté until pale. Next add the chorizo and sauté until the fat runs out into the onion. Stir in the chilli flakes.

Toast the pine nuts in a dry frying pan/skillet for a minute or so until golden. Take care because they will burn easily. Transfer to a plate to cool.

Pulse the garlic, parsley, breadcrumbs and half the pine nuts in a processor until fine. Add to the pan/skillet and let cool.

To make the tomato sauce, heat the oil in a saucepan, add the onion and garlic and sauté until pale gold in colour. Increase the heat, add the sugar and the tomatoes with their juices, then simmer for a few minutes.

Stuff the squid with the cold chorizo mixture and close with a cocktail stick. Heat the remaining oil in a frying pan/skillet, add the stuffed squid and sauté on both sides until pale golden, about 2 minutes on each side. Add to the saucepan and cook in the preheated oven for 15 minutes. Remove from the oven, sprinkle with the coarsley chopped parsley and remaining toasted pine nuts and serve.

Note If you have to clean the squid yourself, first pull off the tentacles. Rinse out the bodies and discard the stiff transparent quill, if any. Cut the tentacles away from the head, and discard the head. Chop the tentacles into small pieces.

stuffed mussels
mejillones rellenos

This is a popular dish on the Madrid tapas bar circuit. It is a great one for entertaining because you can prepare it in advance and it's quick to cook.

12–16 live mussels

100 ml/$\frac{1}{2}$ cup white wine

2 garlic cloves, peeled

1 teaspoon olive oil

1 small onion, finely grated

1 tablespoon finely chopped Serrano ham

1 teaspoon tomato purée/paste

1 teaspoon finely chopped fresh flat leaf parsley

1 egg, beaten with 1 tablespoon water

100 g/$\frac{2}{3}$ cup dried white breadcrumbs

oil, for deep-frying

WHITE SAUCE

25 g/2 tablespoons butter

50 g/$\frac{1}{3}$ cup plain/all-purpose flour

100 ml/scant $\frac{1}{2}$ cup milk

sea salt and freshly ground white pepper

an electric deep-fryer (optional)

SERVES 4

To clean the mussels, scrub them in cold water and pull off the beards. Tap them against a work surface and discard any that don't close.

Put them in a saucepan with the wine and garlic, cover and heat until they open. Remove as soon as they do, and discard any that don't. Remove the mussels from the shells, reserving the shells, and chop the flesh. Strain the cooking liquid through a fine sieve/strainer and reserve it.

Heat the oil in a frying pan/skillet, then add the onion and Serrano ham. Cook for 3 minutes over low heat, then add the tomato paste, parsley, chopped mussels and 2 tablespoons of the reserved mussel liquid. Stir well and cook for 1 minute. Remove from the heat and let cool.

To make the white sauce, melt the butter in a saucepan, add the flour and cook, stirring, for 1 minute to burst the starch grains. Slowly pour in the milk, stirring all the time. Cook over low heat until the sauce is thick. Add salt and pepper to taste and let cool. Clean half the mussel shells and discard the remainder. Put 1 teaspoon of the mussel mixture in each half shell, smoothing the top with the back of a spoon. Put a teaspoon of white sauce on top of each one, then arrange on a plate, cover and chill overnight.

Put the beaten egg in a bowl and the breadcrumbs on a plate. Dip the mussels in the egg, then roll in the breadcrumbs. Fill a saucepan/deep-fryer with oil to the recommended level and heat to 195°C (380°F). Add the mussels in batches and fry until golden. Remove with a slotted spoon and drain on paper towels. Serve immediately.

mussels with fennel alioli
mejillones con alioli

Although you can buy ready-cooked and flavoured, vacuum-packed mussels, it's so much better from both a cost and flavour point of view to buy them really fresh and clean them yourself. Most of their sold weight is shell, but when cooked in a tasty broth and served with bread on the side they are surprisingly filling, and made for sharing. Eating them always creates a lot of mess, but that's all part of the fun.

1 kg/2^1/$_4$ lbs. live mussels

2 small fennel bulbs, with feathery tops intact and reserved for alioli

1 tablespoon olive oil

1 tablespoon butter

1 garlic clove, finely chopped

1 small onion or 2 shallots, finely chopped

125 ml/^{1}/$_2$ cup dry white wine

250 ml/1 cup fish stock/broth

2 ripe tomatoes, diced

a handful of fresh flat leaf parsley, roughly chopped

2 baguettes, to serve

FENNEL ALIOLI

reserved fennel tops (see above)

185 ml/^{2}/$_3$ cup good-quality mayonnaise

3 garlic cloves, crushed

SERVES 4

To clean the mussels, scrub them in cold water and pull off the beards. Tap them against a work surface and discard any mussels that don't close. Drain in a colander and set aside until they are needed.

To make the alioli, finely chop the feathery tops of the fennel and combine in a small bowl with the mayonnaise and garlic. Cover and chill until needed.

Finely chop the fennel bulbs. Heat the oil and butter in a large saucepan set over medium heat and gently cook the garlic, onion and fennel for about 10 minutes until the fennel has softened.

Add the wine, stock/broth and tomatoes and bring to the boil. Cook for 5 minutes. Add the mussels, cover tightly with a lid and cook for a further 5 minutes, shaking the pan occasionally, until the mussels have opened. Discard any that don't open. Add the parsley and stir.

Spoon the mussels into serving bowls and put an empty bowl on the table for discarded shells. Offer the fennel alioli on the side for spooning along with some warmed, sliced baguette.

Next time For a tasty alternative, try adding some finely diced fresh chorizo sausage to the pan when cooking off the garlic, onion and fennel.

baked sardines
sardinas en cazuela

A mixture of very finely chopped vegetables forms the basis of this dish. It can be served either very hot straight from the oven or left until cold, which is perfect in summer. In winter, you could substitute the sardines for fresh herrings instead. In true Spanish style, eat it with bread to mop up the juices.

5 tablespoons/$\frac{1}{3}$ cup extra virgin olive oil

1 red bell pepper, halved, deseeded and finely chopped

2 medium onions, finely chopped

3 garlic cloves, crushed

2 large tomatoes, skinned, deseeded and cut into 3-cm/1-inch cubes

1 teaspoon hot paprika

a pinch of saffron threads

$\frac{1}{4}$ teaspoon ground cumin

2 bay leaves

2 tablespoons chopped fresh flat leaf parsley, plus extra leaves to serve

9–12 fresh sardine fillets (depending on the size of the dish)

fine sea salt and freshly ground black pepper

SERVES 4–6

Heat 3 tablespoons of the oil in a frying pan/skillet, add the red pepper, onions and garlic and cook gently until softened but not coloured, 8–10 minutes. Add the tomatoes, paprika, saffron and its soaking water, cumin and bay leaves and cook for a further 5–8 minutes (add a little water if the mixture sticks to the pan/skillet) until completely cooked. Season with salt and pepper and fold in the parsley.

Preheat the oven to 190°C (375°F) Gas 5.

Put the sardine fillets on a tray skin side down and sprinkle with a little salt and pepper.

Arrange one-third of the fillets skin side up in the ovenproof dish and cover with one-third of the cooked mixture. Repeat twice more – when adding the last layer, let the silver sardine skin peek through. Grind over a little more pepper and spoon over the rest of the oil.

Bake in a preheated oven for 15–20 minutes until sizzling. Sprinkle with parsley leaves, then serve.

cod balls
albóndigas de bacalao

Dried salt cod is known as *bacalao* in Spain. It can be found in specialist food shops. Though Spain is seafood-mad, with fresh fish widely available, salt cod has an almost religious significance. In fact, that is the origin of its popularity in Catholic southern Europe – as a reliable source of fish for the Friday fast. It must be soaked to soften it and to remove most of the salt. You can substitute it with another meaty white fish and halve the cooking time.

125 g/4 oz. boneless salt cod

300 g/10 oz. potatoes

1 bay leaf

1 garlic clove, crushed

1 tablespoon chopped fresh flat leaf parsley

1 egg

plain/all-purpose flour, for coating

freshly ground white pepper

oil, for frying

TO SERVE

lemon wedges (optional)

alioli (page 117) (optional)

an electric deep-fryer (optional)

SERVES 4

To prepare the salt cod, soak it in cold water for 24 hours, changing the water every 4–5 hours. Just before you are ready to use it, drain well.

Prick the potatoes, arrange on a roasting pan then bake in a preheated oven at 200°C (400°F) Gas 6 for 1 hour or until soft. Scoop the flesh out of the skins into a bowl and mash.

Put the cod in a saucepan, cover with cold water, add the bay leaf, bring to the boil and simmer for 30 minutes. Remove from the heat and let cool. Discard the skin and flake the flesh into a bowl, removing all the bones. Add the flesh to the mashed potatoes and stir in the garlic, parsley, pepper and 2 tablespoons of the cod cooking liquid. Roll the mixture into walnut-sized balls. Put in a bowl, cover with clingfilm/plastic wrap and refrigerate for 2–3 hours to firm up.

Crack the egg into a bowl, add 1 tablespoon water and beat lightly. Put the flour on a plate. Dip the cod balls in the beaten egg, then roll in the flour.

Fill a saucepan or deep-fryer one-third full of oil or to the manufacturer's recommended level and heat to 195°C (380°F). Cook the balls, in batches if necessary, for about 3 minutes or until golden brown. Remove with a slotted spoon and drain on paper towels. Serve the cod balls hot, accompanied with alioli or lemon wedges.

salt cod and tuna salad
xató

Xató, pronounced 'chay-toh', was originally a fishermen's salad. The lettuce is traditionally soaked in the sauce for 1 hour, but can be given less time as in this recipe. Spanish salads usually aren't tossed until you dress them yourself at the table, but this is an exception to the rule. Try to get hold of the great Basque white wine Txomin Etxaniz with its briny mineral notes – it's excellent with salt cod.

200 g/8 oz. boneless salt cod

1 head of escarole lettuce or curly endive, leaves separated and kept in cold water for 30 minutes until crisp

3 slightly green tomatoes, cored and cut into wedges

8 anchovy fillets, canned or from a jar

225 g/8 oz. jar of good-quality tuna in olive oil

12 green olives

12 black olives

XATÓ SAUCE

2 dried chillies, about 5 cm/2 inches long, such as Spanish guindillas

4 tablespoons sherry vinegar

1/2 teaspoon sea salt

10 blanched almonds, lightly toasted in a dry frying pan/skillet and chopped

3 garlic cloves, finely chopped

125 ml/1/2 cup extra virgin olive oil

SERVES 6

To prepare the salt cod, soak it in cold water for 24 hours, changing the water every 4–5 hours. Just before you are ready to use it, drain well.

To make the sauce, soak the chillies in boiling water for 15 minutes. Drain, deseed and chop coarsely. Put the chillies, vinegar, salt, almonds and garlic in a blender and pulse to a purée. With the motor running, gradually add the oil. Transfer to a bowl.

Shred the soaked salt cod with your fingers and add to the sauce. Chill for about 30 minutes so that the fish 'cooks' a little in the acidity of the dressing.

Drain the lettuce and pat dry. Add to the sauce and toss gently. Put the tomatoes, anchovies and tuna on top of the lettuce, add the olives and toss just before serving.

peppers stuffed with salt cod
pimientos rellenos de bacalao

Piquillo peppers are grown in the Navarra region in the north of Spain. The word *piquillo* in Spanish means 'little beak'. These peppers are slightly sour and very small, so perfect for tapas. If you cannot get hold of any, substitute them for jarred roasted red peppers or chargrill some red peppers yourself, let cool and discard the blackened skins.

150 g/6 oz. boneless salt cod

200 ml/scant 1 cup milk

1 small onion, finely sliced

2 bay leaves

a sprig of fresh flat leaf parsley

25 g/2 tablespoons unsalted butter

2 tablespoons plain/all-purpose flour

8 canned piquillo peppers, drained

sea salt and freshly ground white pepper

sliced bread, to serve (optional)

SERVES 4

To prepare the salt cod, soak it in cold water for 24 hours, changing the water every 4–5 hours. Just before you are ready to use it, drain well.

Put the milk in a saucepan, then add the onion, bay leaves and parsley. Heat almost to boiling, then remove from the heat and let cool before straining.

Melt the butter in a saucepan, then stir in the flour and cook for 1 minute. Slowly stir in the strained milk. Cook over medium heat for 3 minutes or until the mixture is thick. Season with salt and pepper and let cool.

Put the cod in a saucepan and cover with cold water. Bring to the boil, then simmer for 20 minutes. Remove and pat dry with paper towels. Remove the skin and flake the flesh into a bowl, making sure to remove all the bones. Pour in the white sauce and mix well. Stuff into the cavity of the peppers. Refrigerate for 2 hours or overnight.

Transfer the peppers to an ovenproof dish and cook in a preheated oven at 150°C (300°F) Gas 2 for 15 minutes. Serve in a bowl or on sliced bread.

garlic prawns
gambas al ajillo

Variations of this recipe are found all over Spain. Serve with a very cold fino sherry. It's worth making a double quantity of the alioli and keeping it in the refrigerator to use as an accompaniment to other types of seafood or meat, such as chicken.

48 small uncooked prawns/shrimp, about 600 g/1¼ lb., peeled and deveined, with tail fins left on

4 tablespoons extra virgin olive oil

8 garlic cloves, peeled and bruised

6 small dried chillies

8 small fresh bay leaves

freshly squeezed juice of ½ lemon

sea salt

ALIOLI

5 garlic cloves, finely chopped

a large pinch of salt

100 ml/½ cup extra virgin olive oil

2 teaspoons lemon juice, plus extra to taste

100 ml/½ cup sunflower/safflower oil

fine sea salt and freshly ground white pepper

4 individual cazuelas (terracotta ramekins), 10–12 cm/4–5 inch diameter, preheated in a hot oven

SERVES 4

To make the alioli, pound the garlic and salt to a smooth, thick, creamy consistency with a mortar and pestle. Slowly drip in the olive oil, mixing with the pestle. Switch to a whisk and mix in the lemon juice, pepper and, little by little, half the sunflower/safflower oil. Add 1–2 teaspoons cold water and whisk well while adding the remaining oil. The mixture will be very thick. Set aside for at least 30 minutes for the garlic to mellow, then add extra salt, pepper and lemon juice to taste.

To prepare the prawns/shrimp, put on a plate and sprinkle lightly with salt. Heat the oil in a frying pan/skillet, add the garlic and sauté until brown. Add the chillies, bay leaves and prawns/shrimp all at once and sauté without turning until they are crusted and curled on one side. Then turn them over and crust the other side, about 3½ minutes in total.

Transfer the prawns/shrimp to the preheated cazuelas, sprinkle with the lemon juice and top with a spoonful of alioli. Serve immediately while still bubbling hot.

prawns in overcoats
gambas a la gabardina

This tapas dish goes perfectly with a glass of cold beer. It's a simple recipe and can be whipped up in no time at all. This method of deep-frying will make the batter crisp, while the prawns/shrimp remain tender and juicy inside. Cook them in small batches so as not to reduce the temperature of the oil.

300 g/10 oz. uncooked prawns/shrimp, shell on

125 g/¾ cup plain/all-purpose flour

1 teaspoon baking powder

a pinch of salt

a pinch of oak-smoked sweet Spanish paprika

250 ml/1 cup beer

oil, for frying

lemon wedges, to serve

an electric deep-fryer (optional)

SERVES 4

Peel the prawns/shrimp, but leave the tail fins intact. Sift the flour, baking powder, salt and paprika into a bowl, mix well, then pour in the beer. Let rest for a few minutes.

Fill a saucepan or deep-fryer one-third full of oil or to the manufacturer's recommended level and heat to 195°C (380°F). Dip the prawns/shrimp in the batter, cook in the oil until golden brown, drain on paper towels and serve with lemon wedges on the side.

vegetables

jewelled gazpacho
gazpacho con joyitas

The addition of jewel-like cubes of frozen finely chopped vegetables to the soup instead of the usual ice cubes gives the dish more colour and a little extra flavour.

700 g/1 ¹/₂ lb. fresh ripe tomatoes, cored and quartered

300 ml/1 ¹/₄ cups tomato or V8 juice

1 small garlic clove, crushed

1 medium red bell pepper, halved, deseeded and coarsely chopped

2 spring onions/scallions, trimmed and coarsely chopped

1 cucumber, peeled and coarsely chopped

2 tablespoons chopped fresh coriander/cilantro

2 tablespoons sherry vinegar

1 tablespoon sweet chilli sauce

sea salt and freshly ground black pepper

FROZEN VEGETABLE CUBES

3 tablespoons finely chopped cucumber

3 tablespoons finely chopped red pepper

3 tablespoons finely chopped radishes

3 tablespoons finely chopped tomato

SERVES 6

Put the tomatoes and juice in a blender and whizz until smooth. Pour half into a pitcher. Mix all the remaining vegetables in a bowl. Add half the vegetables to the blender, blend again until smooth and transfer to a bowl. Put the tomato mixture, the remaining vegetables and the coriander/cilantro in the blender, blend until smooth, then add to the bowl. Stir well, then mix in the vinegar and chilli sauce and add salt and pepper to taste. Cover and chill overnight.

To make the frozen vegetable cubes, mix the chopped vegetables together and pack into ice-cube trays. Freeze.

Ladle the soup into chilled bowls or tumblers and put a couple of frozen vegetable cubes in each one.

75

pinchos

Pinchos are little morsels that are usually eaten on an honesty system –
you help yourself to the different varieties on display. Generally, they are eaten
without a plate, and in some bars you are charged according to the
number of cocktail sticks/toothpicks you've used.

2 tablespoons olive oil

1 garlic clove, crushed

$^1/_2$ teaspoon dried chilli/hot red pepper
flakes

leaves from 2 sprigs of fresh thyme,
plus extra to serve

100 g/4 oz. white asparagus, canned or
from a jar

2 tablespoons ground/slivered almonds

$^1/_2$ can pimientos, chopped

8 slices of white bread, lightly toasted

sea salt and freshly ground black pepper

SERVES 4

Put the oil, garlic, chilli/hot red pepper flakes and thyme
in a saucepan, bring to the boil, then remove from the
heat. Let cool, then strain.

Put the asparagus in a blender and pulse until smooth.
Slowly add the strained oil and blend again. Mix in the
ground/slivered almonds and salt and pepper to taste.

Spoon the asparagus mixture onto the sliced bread and
top with the sliced pimiento. Add a few thyme leaves
and serve on a tray for your guests to help themselves.

garlic olive oil, warm marinated olives and serrano ham platter

This sharing plate is simplicity itself to put together and absolutely no preparation is needed once your guests arrive. Lay out the platter and let it sit at room temperature for a short while before serving. It goes very well with a fruity sangría.

GARLIC OLIVE OIL

8 garlic cloves, unpeeled

65 ml/¼ cup light olive oil

65 ml/¼ cup extra virgin olive oil

2 tablespoons balsamic vinegar

WARM MARINATED OLIVES

100 g/4 oz. large green olives

100 g/4 oz. small black olives

250 ml/1 cup extra virgin olive oil

2 sprigs of fresh thyme

2 dried red chillies

1 bay leaf

2 thin slices of orange zest

TO SERVE

8 slices of Serrano ham

crusty bread, to serve

SERVES 6–8

To make the garlic olive oil, put the garlic cloves and light olive oil in a small saucepan and cook over medium heat for 5 minutes. Remove from the heat and let cool. Add the extra virgin olive oil and vinegar and transfer to a serving bowl.

Put the olives in a small, heatproof bowl. Put the oil, thyme, chillies, bay leaf and orange zest in a small saucepan. Set over medium heat. As soon as you hear the herbs starting to sizzle in the oil, remove the pan from the heat and pour the mixture over the olives. Let cool for 20 minutes.

To serve, arrange the still-warm garlic oil, olives, Serrano ham and bread on a platter and let your guests help themselves.

artichokes with serrano ham
alcachofas con jamón serrano

For this recipe, you need the tiny, often purplish-green variety of artichoke, available in early summer before it develops the hairy choke above the heart. Serve this dish with a crisp sherry such as a manzanilla, from the seaside town of Sanlúcar de Barrameda.

1 lemon, halved

750 g/1½ lb. very small artichokes

4 tablespoons extra virgin olive oil

8 slices of Serrano ham, chopped

3 tablespoons chopped fresh
flat leaf parsley

coarse sea salt and freshly ground
black pepper

SERVES 4

Fill a saucepan with water and squeeze in the lemon juice. Add the squeezed halves of lemon and some salt.

Trim the stalk of each artichoke to 1 cm/½ inch, then trim off all the outer leaves until you reach the tender inner leaves. Cut the artichoke in half lengthways. As you prepare them, add to the pan of lemon water to stop them turning brown.

Bring to the boil, then lower the heat and simmer for about 7 minutes until just tender. Drain and dry.

Heat the oil in a frying pan/skillet, add the artichokes cut side down and sauté for 5 minutes. Turn them over and sauté the other side for a further 2 minutes. Add the Serrano ham and cook for a further 4 minutes until crisp and golden. Sprinkle with the parsley and pepper and serve.

artichoke hearts marinated in garlic
corazones de alcachofa macerados con ajo

Artichokes are easier to cook than you might think. Just make sure you remove as many of the green leaves as possible because they can be tough. As you prepare them, put them in a bowl of cold water with a squeeze of lemon juice to stop them discolouring, and don't be afraid of overcooking them.

8 small artichokes

freshly squeezed juice of 1 lemon and grated zest of $\frac{1}{2}$ unwaxed lemon

3 tablespoons olive oil

6 garlic cloves, peeled

a sprig of fresh thyme

2 tablespoons Spanish red wine vinegar

a sprig of fresh flat leaf parsley

sea salt and freshly ground white pepper

SERVES 4

Cut off the artichoke stalks 1 cm/$\frac{1}{2}$ inch from the base. Trim off the outer leaves and, using a potato peeler, peel the outer sections and remove the green leaves. Cut off the tip and spoon out any furry bits from the middle section (this is called the choke). As you prepare them, put them in a bowl of cold water with the lemon juice.

Bring a saucepan of salted water to the boil, add the artichoke hearts and cook until tender, about 20 minutes. Meanwhile put the oil, garlic, thyme and lemon zest in a small saucepan and heat gently. Remove from the heat and leave to infuse. Drain the artichokes, cut in half and dry on paper towels. Transfer to a bowl, then add the garlic oil, the vinegar and parsley and stir well. Sprinkle with salt and pepper, cover and let marinate in the refrigerator for 2–3 days. Serve at room temperature.

marinated black olives

Oily black olives are the best variety for this recipe because their soft texture and residual oil suit the spicy, sharp flavours of the marinade. Marinate for as long as possible – at least a month. They will keep for several months; just mix and taste occasionally.

500 g/about 1 lb. black Spanish olives in brine

4 garlic cloves, sliced

2 dried red chillies

8 black peppercorns

1 slice of lemon

4 sprigs of fresh flat leaf parsley

4 fresh bay leaves

a pinch of salt

300 ml/1¼ cups red wine vinegar

SERVES 4

Drain the olives of their brine, reserving a little for refilling. Put the olives in a bowl and add the garlic, chillies, peppercorns, lemon, parsley, bay leaves and salt. Mix, then transfer to a jar into which they just fit and pour over the vinegar and the reserved brine. Shake well and let marinate at room temperature for at least 2 weeks.

marinated green olives

Use firm green olives for this recipe. The crunchy texture remains during marinating. This mixture of flavours is typical of Andalusia. Most of Spain's green olives grow in this region – just a whiff of these olives will transport you to southern Spain.

500 g/about 1 lb. large green Spanish olives in brine, drained

6 garlic cloves, sliced

1 tablespoon coriander seeds, lightly crushed

1 tablespoon fennel seeds, lightly crushed

6 sprigs of fresh thyme, bruised

4 sprigs of fresh rosemary, bruised

grated zest and freshly squeezed juice of 1 unwaxed orange

olive oil

SERVES 4

Put the olives in a bowl with the garlic, coriander, fennel, thyme, rosemary and orange zest and juice. Stir, then transfer to a glass jar into which they just fit. Cover with olive oil, shake well and let marinate at room temperature for at least 6 days.

salted almonds

Almond trees were brought to Spain by the Moors and flourished, especially around Seville, where salted almonds feature regularly in tapas bars.

olive oil

200 g/2 cups whole blanched almonds

1 teaspoon coarse salt or sea salt, finely ground

$^1/_2$ teaspoon oak-smoked sweet Spanish paprika

SERVES 4

Pour a 2-cm/1-inch depth of oil into a saucepan and heat to 195°C (380°F). Test with a sugar thermometer or drop in a small cube of bread – it should turn golden in about 30 seconds.

Sauté the almonds until lightly golden. Drain, sprinkle with the salt and paprika and mix well. Let cool slightly before serving.

grilled wild asparagus
espárragos trigueros a la plancha

Asparagus served with *salsa mayonesa* (fresh mayonnaise), *sel marina* (coarse sea salt) and *choricitos fritos* (sautéed sliced baby chorizos) is a simple dish. True wild asparagus grows on the edges of wheatfields in spring and is called *trigueros* after *trigo*, the Spanish word for 'wheat'. Sweet in flavour, it is a much paler green than our thin asparagus.

750 g/1½ lb. thin asparagus

3 tablespoons olive oil

a pinch of fine sea salt

freshly ground black pepper

MAYONESA

1 garlic clove, finely chopped

2 teaspoons freshly squeezed lemon juice

a pinch of fine sea salt

1 egg yolk

150 ml/²⁄₃ cup olive oil

TO SERVE

coarse sea salt

2 baby chorizos (choricitos), sliced, then fried without oil in a dry frying pan/skillet

SERVES 4

To make the mayonesa, put the garlic, half the lemon juice, salt and a few drops of water in a mortar and pound to a paste. Add the egg yolk, grinding with the pestle in one direction. Gradually mix in the oil in drops. After adding 100 ml/½ cup, add a little more of the lemon juice and continue slowly mixing in the oil until a thick emulsion forms. Taste and adjust the flavour with more salt and the remaining lemon juice if needed. Alternatively, use a blender or small food processor, but you will have to double the ingredients or the mixture won't cover the blades. Cover any leftovers with clingfilm/plastic wrap, chill and keep for another use.

Trim the asparagus and peel away the papery triangular bits from the stalk. Put the oil, salt and pepper in a shallow dish, add the asparagus and turn to coat.

Heat a ridged stove-top grill pan until smoking. Add the asparagus, a batch at a time, turning the spears over when grill marks appear. They will take 1½–2½ minutes on each side. Serve while still hot with the mayonesa, sea salt and chorizos in small bowls.

marinated peppers
pimientos picantes

Marinated peppers are very simple but taste fantastic; for the best result, use small peppers. Serve on a slice of bread or toast, or go that bit further and serve the bread old-fashioned tapas-style on top of a glass of chilled sherry.

3 small red bell peppers

3 tablespoons olive oil

50 ml/¼ cup sherry vinegar

a sprig of fresh thyme

a sprig of fresh rosemary

2 garlic cloves, sliced

½ teaspoon cayenne pepper

1 tablespoon salted capers, rinsed and drained

1 tablespoon chopped fresh flat leaf parsley

sea salt and freshly ground white pepper

thinly sliced bread, to serve

SERVES 4

Grill the peppers slowly under a preheated overhead grill/broiler until the skins are blistered and black. Transfer to a plastic bag, seal and let steam. When cool enough to handle, pull off the skins and remove the seeds and membranes. Put the peppers in a sieve/strainer set over a bowl to catch the juices and cut into 1-cm/½-inch strips.

Heat a heavy-based frying pan/skillet, then add the oil, vinegar, thyme, rosemary, garlic, cayenne pepper and the collected pepper juices. Cook over low heat for 2 minutes. Add the peppers, capers, parsley and salt and pepper to taste. Cook, stirring, for 1 minute. Remove from the heat and let cool. Transfer to a bowl, cover and chill overnight.

When ready to eat, return to room temperature and serve on a thin slice of bread with sherry, wine or beer. This dish can be kept in the refrigerator for up to one week.

spanish stuffed peppers
piquillos rellenos

This vegetarian tapas dish is full of flavour. Why not serve it alongside the artichoke hearts marinated in garlic (page 83), sautéed lentils with mushrooms (page 100) and patatas bravas (page 112) for a delicious vegetarian medley of tapas?

185 g/6 oz. canned piquillo peppers or pimientos

4 tablespoons olive oil

3–4 garlic cloves, chopped

550 g/2 cups canned white beans, such as cannellini beans, part-drained, reserving the liquid

2 tablespoons sherry vinegar (optional)

a handful of fresh thyme or mint, chopped

a handful of baby salad greens, such as spinach, watercress or flat leaf parsley

sea salt and freshly ground black pepper

SERVES 4

Drain the piquillo peppers and pat dry with paper towels.

Heat the oil, garlic and part-drained white beans in a non-stick frying pan/skillet and mash with a fork to a thick, coarse purée. Add 1 tablespoon of the vinegar, if using, and 1 tablespoon of the reserved bean liquid, stir, then season well with salt and pepper. Let cool slightly, then stuff each piquillo with the mixture and sprinkle with the thyme.

Add some salad greens and trickle over a tablespoon of the reserved bean liquid and a few drops of vinegar, if using, before serving.

Variation Instead of piquillos, use 4 sweet red peppers, halved lengthways and deseeded. Grill/broil them skin side up until blistered and black. Transfer to a plastic bag, seal and let steam. When cool enough to handle, rub off the skins, stuff with the mixture, roll up, then serve as in the main recipe.

spanish tart with peppers
coca con pimientos

A coca is an open empanada, a bit like a pizza, that originates in Catalonia and the Balearics. It is cooked in a communal outdoor stone or brick oven. A typical coca has just one or two topping ingredients, as in this recipe. If you haven't any piquillo peppers, use canned pimientos or grilled or roasted fresh red peppers.

250 g/1²/₃ cups plain/all-purpose flour

¹/₂ sachet easy-blend/active dried yeast

¹/₂ teaspoon fine sea salt

TOPPING

4 tablespoons extra virgin olive oil

2 large red onions, cut into wedges

about 500 g/1lb. canned piquillo peppers, drained

leaves from a small handful of fresh rosemary sprigs or fresh thyme

2 tablespoons anchovy paste or purée, or canned anchovies, chopped and mashed

16 marinated anchovy fillets

a baking sheet, oiled

SERVES 4–6

To make the dough, put the flour, yeast and salt in a bowl and mix. Add 150 ml/²/₃ cup lukewarm water and mix to a satiny dough, then knead using a little extra flour, still in the bowl for 5 minutes or until silky. Cover the bowl with a cloth and leave in a warm place for about 1 hour or until the dough has doubled in size.

Meanwhile, to make the topping, heat 3 tablespoons of the oil in a frying pan/skillet, add the onions and cook, stirring over medium heat, until softened and transparent. Slice half the piquillos and add to the pan. Stir in most of the rosemary.

Preheat the oven to 220°C (425°F) Gas 7.

Transfer the dough to the oiled baking sheet. Punch down, flatten and roll out the dough to a circle 30 cm/12 inches in diameter. Snip, twist or roll the edges. Spread the anchovy paste all over the top. Add the remaining piquillos, left whole, and the cooked onion mixture. Arrange the anchovies and remaining rosemary in a decorative pattern on top and sprinkle with the remaining oil.

Bake in the preheated oven for 25–30 minutes until the base is crisp and risen, the edges golden and the filling hot and wilted. Serve in wedges, hot or cool.

spanish flatbread
coca mallorquina

This recipe is a twist on the traditional coca as it has a few more toppings than is customary. Serve with a medium-bodied, soft red, such as Rioja.

300 g/2 cups strong white bread flour

1 sachet easy-blend/active dried yeast

a pinch of sugar

1½ teaspoons fine sea salt

2 teaspoons olive oil

TOPPING

2 garlic cloves, crushed to a paste with salt

6 tablespoons extra virgin olive oil

4 large tomatoes, cores cut out with a small sharp knife and the flesh very finely sliced

2 courgettes/zucchini, finely sliced

4 tablespoons pine nuts

16 black olives

sea salt and freshly ground black pepper

1–2 baking sheets, oiled

SERVES 4–6

Put the flour in a bowl and mix in the yeast, sugar and salt. Make a hollow in the centre.

Put 250 ml/1 cup hand-hot water in a bowl and mix in the oil. Pour into the hollow in the flour, then mix with your hands until the dough comes away from the bowl. If it seems too dry, add more water, about 1 tablespoon. Transfer to a lightly floured surface and knead for 5 minutes until smooth.

Put the ball of dough in an oiled bowl, cover with clingfilm/plastic wrap and set aside in a warm place for about 1 hour or until doubled in size.

Preheat the oven to 220°C (425°F) Gas 7.

Cut half the dough out of the bowl, put on a lightly floured work surface and knead to a flattened ball. Re-cover the bowl. Using a floured rolling pin, roll out to a rectangle about 30 x 20 cm x 5 mm/12 x 8 inches x ⅛ inch thick. Transfer to an oiled baking sheet and roll up the edge a to make a border.

To make the topping, mix the crushed garlic with 1 tablespoon of the oil and smear half the mixture over the dough. Put half the tomato and courgette/zucchini slices on top, sprinkle with half the pine nuts, salt and pepper, then drizzle with 2 tablespoons of the oil. Bake in the preheated oven for 10 minutes. Dot with half the olives and return to the oven for about 5 minutes or until golden and cooked.

Repeat with the other piece of dough and the remaining topping ingredients.

spanish roasted vegetables
escalivada

This dish of summer or autumn vegetables roasted to sweetness is deceptively simple. Its success depends on excellent olive oil and vegetables cooked in their skins for extra flavour. You can add fragments of salt cod, capers, olives or even cubes of goats' cheese to your liking. Different herbs can be added at serving time and even a few drops of vinegar, but on the whole, simplicity is best. Excellent with a fruity white, a rosé or even fino sherry.

2 red bell peppers

2 yellow or orange bell peppers

2 red onions, unpeeled

2 whole garlic heads

6–8 tablespoons/$^1/_3$-$^1/_2$ cup first cold-pressed extra virgin olive oil

4 slices of butternut squash or pumpkin, about 1.5 cm/$^1/_2$ inch thick, deseeded if necessary, or 2 large courgettes/zucchini, halved lengthways and scored with a fork

2 baby aubergines/eggplant or 1 large, sliced lengthways and scored with a fork

1 small handful of fresh herbs, such as parsley, oregano, mint and thyme

sea salt and freshly ground black pepper

1–2 roasting pans

SERVES 4

Preheat the oven to 250°C (475°F) Gas 9.

Leave the stalks on the peppers, but remove and discard the pith and seeds. Cut the unpeeled onions almost in half crossways, leaving one side joined, as a hinge.

Cut the unpeeled heads of garlic almost in half crossways, leaving a hinge of papery skin. Pour a teaspoon of the oil over the cut surfaces of the garlic, then put the bulbs back together again. Wrap up in foil, to make 2 packets.

Arrange all of the prepared vegetables, including the butternut squash and aubergines/eggplant, in a single layer in the roasting pan(s), cut sides uppermost. Sprinkle with 3–4 tablespoons of the oil.

Roast in the preheated oven for 35–40 minutes until soft and fragrant. Transfer to a serving dish, sprinkle with the herbs, salt and pepper and the remaining oil. Serve the vegetables hot or warm.

vegetable sauté
pisto manchego

Pisto Manchego, from La Mancha in the heart of Spain, is probably based on an earlier Moorish aubergine/eggplant dish. The original didn't include tomatoes or peppers because these foods weren't introduced from the New World until the 16th century, after the expulsion of the Moors. This dish is very good eaten cold, but also works well warm – try serving it with a poached egg on top to add a different texture.

150 ml/^{2}/$_3$ cup extra virgin olive oil

2 onions, chopped

4 garlic cloves, finely chopped

^{1}/$_2$ teaspoon cumin seeds

2 medium aubergines/eggplant, chopped into 1-cm/^{1}/$_2$-inch cubes

6 tomatoes, skinned, deseeded and chopped, reserving any juices

300 g/10 oz. courgettes/zucchini, cut into 1-cm/^{1}/$_2$-inch cubes

3 large roasted red bell peppers from a jar, cut into 1-cm/^{1}/$_2$-inch cubes

1 tablespoon coarsely chopped fresh oregano, plus extra leaves to serve

2 teaspoons sherry vinegar or red wine vinegar

sea salt and freshly ground black pepper

SERVES 4–6

Heat half the oil in a heavy saucepan, add the onions and garlic and over medium heat for 5 minutes until softened. Remove to a bowl. Increase the heat, add the remaining oil, cumin and aubergines/eggplant, stir until they take up the oil and soften slightly, then add the tomatoes and their juices. Simmer until the mixture starts to thicken.

Fold in the courgettes/zucchini, peppers and chopped oregano, season with salt and pepper and simmer gently, uncovered, until soft. Fold in the vinegar and serve hot or cold with the oregano leaves sprinkled over.

sautéed lentils with mushrooms
lentejas salteadas con setas

Small brown lentils work well in this recipe because they stay firm during cooking, but the big green ones called castellanas have a good flavour too. You can make this dish vegetarian by simply omitting the bacon from the recipe.

250 g/1¼ cups small brown lentils, rinsed

3 tablespoons extra virgin olive oil

1 onion, finely chopped

1 garlic clove, crushed

25 g/2 tablespoons butter

100 g/4 oz. small chestnut/cremini mushrooms

100 g/4 oz. oyster mushrooms, halved if large

3 tablespoons chopped fresh flat leaf parsley

1 teaspoon freshly squeezed lemon juice

fine sea salt and freshly ground black pepper

TO SERVE

6–12 slices of streaky bacon

leaves from a small bunch of flat leaf parsley, half chopped, the rest left whole

SERVES 6

Put the lentils in a saucepan, cover with 1 litre/1 quart cold water and bring to the boil. Lower the heat and simmer for about 35 minutes or until tender (the time will depend on the age of the lentils). Drain well.

Heat 2 tablespoons of the oil in a frying pan/skillet, add the onion and garlic and sauté for about 10 minutes until soft and pale golden. Add the butter, the remaining oil and mushrooms. Stir-fry until the mushrooms are just cooked. Add the lentils, chopped parsley, lemon juice, salt and pepper and continue to stir until heated through.

Meanwhile, grill/broil the bacon until crisp. Serve the lentils topped with the parsley and 1–2 slices of bacon per serving.

Variations
• Add 150 g/6 oz. cubed Spanish panceta instead of the mushrooms.
• Add 4 skinned, deseeded and chopped tomatoes instead of the mushrooms.

mushrooms in garlic sauce
champiñones al ajillo

Brown chestnut mushrooms work particularly well in this dish, but you can use other seasonal varieties. The amount of garlic you choose to add is very much up to you: add more if you wish. This dish can be made in advance as it reheats well. You can spoon the mushrooms onto some toasted bread and serve it as a pincho.

125 g/4 oz. small to medium mushrooms

1 tablespoon olive oil

4 garlic cloves, thinly sliced

$\frac{1}{2}$ red chilli, deseeded and finely sliced

50 ml/$\frac{1}{4}$ cup dry sherry

3 tablespoons chicken stock/broth

a pinch of oak-smoked sweet Spanish paprika

sea salt and freshly ground white pepper

SERVES 4

Cut the larger mushrooms in half and set aside. Heat the oil in a heavy-based frying pan/skillet and add all the mushrooms, garlic and chilli. Toss to coat with the oil, then cook for 2 minutes. Add the sherry, stock/broth and a pinch of paprika, cook for a further 2 minutes, then season to taste. Serve the mushrooms warm.

stuffed mushrooms
champiñones rellenos

These colourful stuffed mushrooms make an eye-catching addition to any tapas spread. Bear in mind that this recipe needs some forward planning as the stuffing needs to be left to marinate in the refrigerator overnight.

8 medium mushrooms

2 tablespoons milk

2 tablespoons fresh breadcrumbs

2 tablespoons finely chopped onion

1 garlic clove, crushed

1 tablespoon chopped fresh
flat leaf parsley

2 tablespoons minced pork

1 tablespoon Serrano ham,
finely chopped

1 tablespoon canned chopped
pimiento

1 tablespoon freshly squeezed
lemon juice

olive oil

SERVES 4

Clean the mushrooms and remove the stalks. Finely chop 2 of the stalks and put them in a bowl. Add the milk and breadcrumbs and let soak for 10 minutes.

Add the onion, garlic, parsley, minced pork and Serrano ham. Mix well, cover with clingfilm/plastic wrap and let marinate in the refrigerator overnight.

Preheat the oven to 180°C (350°F) Gas 4. Put the mushroom caps in an ovenproof dish and fill each with 1 heaped teaspoon of the mixture. Swirl over a little olive oil, then cook in a preheated oven for 15 minutes.

Remove from the oven, add a little chopped pimiento to each one and sprinkle with lemon juice. Serve warm.

spinach with pine nuts and raisins
espinacas con piñones y pasas

This dish is frequently found in Catalonia and Andalusia. It is Moorish in origin.
Feel free to add some onion or minced Serrano ham to the dish.

50 g/¹/₂ cup raisins

2 tablespoons olive oil

25 g/¹/₂ cup pine nuts, toasted in a dry frying pan/skillet

2 garlic cloves, sliced

3 tablespoons dry sherry

200 g/8 oz. spinach

a pinch of oak-smoked sweet Spanish paprika

sea salt and freshly ground black pepper

SERVES 4

Soak the raisins in warm water for 3 minutes. Drain.

Heat the oil in a frying pan/skillet, add the pine nuts and garlic and cook for 1 minute. Add the sherry and boil for 1 minute.

Add the spinach and paprika and toss well to coat with the juices. Cook over low heat for 5 minutes. Add the drained raisins with salt and pepper to taste, then serve.

potatoes in shirts
patatas en camisa

Potatoes were introduced from the New World in the early 16th century and are now more of a staple in the Spanish kitchen than almost any other ingredient. They are usually either fried in oil until crisp or cooked in stock, so this recipe is a combination of the two methods.

500 g/1 lb. potatoes

a pinch of saffron threads

2 eggs

1 tablespoon milk

70 g/½ cup plain/all-purpose flour, seasoned with salt and pepper

1 large onion, finely chopped

2 tablespoons chopped fresh flat leaf parsley

250 ml/1 cup hot clear chicken stock/broth

coarse sea salt and freshly ground black pepper

olive oil, for deep-frying, plus 2 tablespoons for sautéing

an electric deep-fryer (optional)

SERVES 4

Cut the potatoes into 1-cm/½-inch slices and put in a bowl of cold water to prevent them from discolouring.

Crush the saffron with a little salt in a pestle and mortar. Put in a bowl, along with the eggs, milk, salt and pepper and whisk well to combine.

Drain the potato slices, pat dry with paper towels and dip them first in the seasoned flour, then in the egg mixture.

Fill a saucepan or deep-fryer one-third full with oil, or to the manufacturer's recommended level. Heat to 195°C (380°F).

Fry the potatoes, a batch at a time, until golden – they don't have to cook through. Remove and drain on paper towels.

Preheat the oven to 200°C (400°F) Gas 6.

Meanwhile, heat the 2 tablespoons oil in a frying pan/skillet, add the onion and sauté until soft and pale golden. Transfer to a casserole. Add the potatoes to the casserole, season with salt and pepper, sprinkle with half the parsley, then add the hot stock. Grind some extra pepper over the top and bake, uncovered, in the preheated oven until the potatoes are tender and the stock has been absorbed.

Sprinkle with the remaining parsley, then serve.

potato fritters with chorizo
buñuelos de patatas con chorizo

These tasty little fritters require just a handful of low-cost ingredients. Serve this dish very hot, with lots of napkins, cocktail sticks/toothpicks, a bowl of coarse sea salt and a copita or two of chilled manzanilla sherry.

500 g/1 lb. potatoes, peeled and cut lengthways into thick fingers

1 tablespoon self-raising/rising flour

2 eggs, separated, plus 1 egg white

100 g/4 oz. cooked chorizo, skinned and chopped into small pieces

sea salt and freshly ground black pepper

olive or sunflower/safflower oil, for deep-frying

wooden cocktail sticks/toothpicks

an electric deep-fryer (optional)

MAKES ABOUT 24

Boil the potatoes in a saucepan of salted water until soft, drain through a colander and cover with a cloth for about 5 minutes to let them dry out. Transfer to a bowl, mash in the flour and season with a little pepper. Mix in the egg yolks, then stir in the chorizo.

Put the egg whites in a separate bowl and whisk until soft peaks form. Fold into the mashed potatoes a little at a time.

Fill a saucepan or deep-fryer one-third full with oil or to the manufacturer's recommended level. Heat to 195°C (380°F).

Preheat the oven to 180°C (350°F) Gas 4.

Working in batches of 6, take heaped teaspoons of the mixture and lower into the hot oil. Fry each batch for 3 minutes until evenly golden, turning them over halfway through (if they brown too quickly they will not have a good texture in the centre). Keep the oil temperature constant. Drain each batch when it is ready on paper towels and keep them warm in the preheated oven until you have cooked the remaining fritters.

Serve hot with wooden cocktail sticks/toothpicks.

potatoes in tomato sauce
patatas bravas

This tapas dish is extremely popular and is served across Spain. It is simple to prepare and makes a good accompaniment to more complicated dishes. The orange zest is a hidden flavour that works well with the tomatoes and chilli.

3 tablespoons olive oil

600 g/1¼ lb. potatoes, cut into 2-cm/¾-inch cubes

1 small onion, grated

3 garlic cloves, crushed

2 tablespoons fino sherry

125 g/4 oz. canned chopped tomatoes

½ teaspoon dried chilli/hot red pepper flakes, well crushed

½ teaspoon freshly grated orange zest

1 teaspoon sugar

1 tablespoon chopped fresh flat leaf parsley

1 fresh bay leaf

SERVES 4

Heat 2 tablespoons of the oil in a frying pan/skillet, add the potatoes and mix well until they are coated in the oil. Cook for 15 minutes until golden brown.

Meanwhile, heat the remaining oil in another frying pan/skillet, add the onion and cook gently for 5 minutes. Add the garlic and sherry, then simmer for 1 minute to burn off the alcohol. Reduce the heat and add the tomatoes, chilli/hot red pepper flakes, orange zest, sugar, parsley and bay leaf. Cook for 10 minutes – add water to stop the mixture thickening too much.

Transfer the cooked potatoes to a serving bowl, pour over the tomato sauce and mix well. This can be made a day in advance and reheated before serving.

cheese and eggs

alioli

Alioli is the garlic-laden version of the Spanish mayonnaise, mahonesa, thought to have originated in Mahon, the capital of the island of Menorca. To help stop it separating, have all the ingredients at room temperature, perhaps slightly warming the oil first. It goes particularly well with chicken and seafood.

4–6 garlic cloves, crushed

1 egg

1 egg yolk

1 teaspoon freshly squeezed lemon juice

500 ml/2 cups olive oil

sea salt and freshly ground black pepper

SERVES 4

Put the garlic, whole egg, egg yolk and lemon juice in a food processor. Blend until pale yellow. Keeping the motor running, slowly pour in the oil, a little at a time. Blend well until thick and silky, then add salt and pepper to taste. Serve at room temperature with fish or meat.

Alioli with potatoes

Put 500 g/1 lb. unpeeled new potatoes in a saucepan, cover with cold water, add a pinch of salt and boil until tender. Drain and let cool. Slip off the skins, cut the potatoes into bite-sized pieces, then serve with the alioli as a dip.

cheese balls
delicias de queso

Manchego cheese is popular all over Spain. It is to the Spanish what Parmesan is to the Italians. The mix of Manchego sheep's cheese and Spanish goats' cheese balances each other perfectly. It will be a real treat for your guests.

2 tablespoons plain/all-purpose flour

2 tablespoons milk

1/2 teaspoon oak-smoked sweet Spanish paprika

1 egg

1 garlic clove, crushed

150 g/6 oz. Manchego cheese, finely grated

150 g/6 oz. soft goats' cheese, preferably Spanish

2 egg whites

1 teaspoon chopped fresh thyme leaves

1 tablespoon Serrano ham, finely chopped

sea salt and freshly ground white pepper

oil, for frying

wooden cocktail sticks/toothpicks

an electric deep-fryer (optional)

SERVES 4

Put the flour and milk in a bowl and stir until smooth. Add the paprika, salt, pepper and the whole egg. Add the garlic and both cheeses and mix well.

Put the egg whites in a bowl and whisk until stiff. Fold one-third into the flour mixture and mix well, then gently fold in the remaining egg whites, taking care not to lose all of the air. Sprinkle with the thyme and Serrano ham.

Fill a saucepan or deep-fryer one-third full of oil or to the manufacturer's recommended level and heat to 195°C (380°F). Using a teaspoon, run the spoon through the mixture, collecting an even amount of thyme and Serrano ham, and drop a heaped spoonful into the hot oil. Cook for 3 minutes or until the mixture is golden brown. Drain on paper towels and serve immediately with wooden cocktail sticks/toothpicks.

fried cheese
queso frito

Queso frito is best eaten hot, straight from the pan. Manchego, hailing from La Mancha, is either semi-cured, ripe or aged with a basket-weave-patterned rind in shades from the palest ochre to deep dark brown and black. Queso frito is one of the most popular tapas, perfect with manzanilla or fino sherry, or with Valdepeñas, a red wine from La Mancha. Serve it with membrillo (quince paste) or mixed olives.

275–300 g/8–10 oz. semi-cured Manchego cheese, 3 months old

2 tablespoons plain/all-purpose flour

1 egg, beaten

150 g/2 cups lightly dried fine fresh white breadcrumbs

150 ml/²⁄₃ cup olive oil

a pinch of oak-smoked sweet Spanish paprika

TO SERVE (OPTIONAL)

membrillo (quince paste)

mixed olives

SERVES 6

Cut all the rind off the Manchego and cut the cheese into 1-cm/½-inch wedges.

Put the flour on a small plate, the beaten egg in a shallow dish and the breadcrumbs on another plate. Working in batches of 6, dip each wedge in the flour, then in the beaten egg, then in the breadcrumbs.

Heat half the oil in a non-stick frying pan/skillet over medium heat, then fry the wedges in batches until golden – about 45 seconds each side. Drain on paper towels.

Wipe out the pan (to get rid of any burned breadcrumbs) and fry the remaining batches in the same way.

Sprinkle with the paprika and serve with membrillo or olives, if using.

Note Membrillo is a thick paste made from quinces, a golden fruit related to the apple and pear, available in autumn. Quinces are cooked into desserts, jellies or jams, and into this sweetly smoky paste. Membrillo is also served with a good Manchego cheese instead of dessert.

aubergine cheese fritters
berenjenas con queso

This tapas dish is sometimes found in bars in Barcelona and elsewhere in Spain served with the local rosé or red wine, well chilled; a delicious combination. If you can't find Cabrales, use mature Cheddar.

1 large aubergine/eggplant, about 350 g/12 oz.

150–200 g/6–7 oz. strong, meltable cheese, such as Cabrales or Cheddar

100 g/²⁄₃ cup plain/all-purpose flour, seasoned with salt and pepper

2 eggs, well beaten with a fork

about 500 ml/2 cups virgin olive or sunflower/safflower oil, for frying

SALSA

2 medium vine-ripened tomatoes, chopped

4 tablespoons/¼ cup chilli oil or olive oil mixed with ½ teaspoon Tabasco sauce

4 teaspoons red wine vinegar or sherry vinegar

12 fresh basil leaves

sea salt and freshly ground black pepper

wooden cocktail sticks/toothpicks

an electric deep-fryer (optional)

SERVES 4

Using a sharp, serrated knife, cut the aubergine/eggplant crossways into 18–24 thin slices about 5 mm/¼ inch thick. Slice the cheese into pieces of the same thickness. Cut and piece them together to fit, sandwiching a piece of cheese between 2 pieces of aubergine/eggplant. To keep the 'sandwiches' closed during cooking, push a cocktail stick, at an angle, through each one.

Put the flour on a plate. Pour the beaten eggs into a shallow dish. Dip the aubergine/eggplant 'sandwiches' first into the flour, then into the beaten eggs, then in flour again to coat.

Fill a saucepan or deep-fryer one-third full of oil or to the manufacturer's recommended level and heat to 195°C (380°F). Slide some of the prepared 'sandwiches' into the hot oil in batches of 3 and fry for 2–3 minutes on the first side. Using tongs, turn and cook for 1–2 minutes on the other side or until golden and crispy, with the cheese melting inside. Drain on paper towels while you coat and cook the rest.

Meanwhile, to make the salsa, put the tomatoes, chilli oil, vinegar, basil leaves, salt and pepper in a food processor. Pulse in brief bursts to a coarse mixture.

Serve the fritters hot with a trickle of the salsa, or with a little pot of salsa as a dip.

baked eggs flamenco style
huevos a la flamenca

This dish earned its name from the riot of colours at work on the plate. You can choose different vegetables to the ones listed here to make the most of what's in season or in your kitchen. This tapas dish is quite substantial, so serve it alongside some lighter dishes such as chicken with garlic (page 11) and pinchos (page 76).

4 tablespoons/¼ cup olive oil

1 onion, finely chopped

1 garlic clove, crushed

125 g /4 oz. cubed Spanish panceta or Italian pancetta

8 tomatoes, skinned, deseeded and chopped

½ teaspoon sweet Spanish paprika

1 tablespoon dry sherry

2 large roasted red bell peppers from a jar or can, cut into cubes

12 asparagus tips, cooked

50 g/½ cup peas, blanched

4 very fresh eggs

8 very thin slices of large cured chorizo, about 35 g/1½ oz.

coarse sea salt and freshly ground black pepper

a frying pan/skillet with an ovenproof handle

a large cazuela (terracotta dish), about 20 cm/8 inches diameter, or 4 small ones (optional)

SERVES 4

Heat the oil in a frying pan/skillet with an ovenproof handle, add the onion and garlic and sauté over medium heat for about 7 minutes until soft and just starting to turn golden. Add the panceta and sauté for 3 minutes. Add the tomatoes, paprika and sherry and cook for about 7 minutes until slightly thickened. Season with a little salt and pepper.

Preheat the oven to 200°C (400°F) Gas 6.

Fold the roasted peppers, asparagus tips and peas into the mixture. (If finishing in a cazuela, transfer the vegetables to the dish at this point.) Make 4 indentations in the mixture and break in the eggs, swirl the white part slightly and leave the yolks whole. Bake in the preheated oven for about 10 minutes until the eggs have just set.

Meanwhile, heat a second small frying pan/skillet and dry-sauté the chorizo on both sides until the oil runs out and the edges are slightly browned. Put on top of the dish and serve.

Note The Spanish method for seasoning a terracotta cazuela is to submerge it in water for 12 hours, then rub several peeled cloves of garlic over the unglazed base. When the juices have been absorbed into the terracotta, fill the cazuela with water and 100 ml/½ cup vinegar and put on top of the stove with a heat-diffusing mat underneath. Bring to the boil slowly and simmer until the liquid has reduced to about 100 ml/½ cup. Let cool and rinse. The cazuela is ready to use.

baked mushrooms with manchego béchamel
champiñones al horno

Look for mushrooms that will be two to three small mouthfuls in size when cooked –
wild field mushrooms or the large portobello mushrooms are both ideal.
These are very rich, so combine them with lighter tapas dishes such as
marinated sardines (page 39) or pinchos (page 76).

2 teaspoons butter

2 teaspoons plain/all-purpose flour

125 ml/½ cup whole milk

50 g/½ cup Manchego cheese, finely grated

12 wide, flat field mushrooms

¼ teaspoon oak-smoked sweet Spanish paprika

FENNEL SALAD

1 small fennel bulb

a handful of fresh flat leaf parsley leaves

2 teaspoons olive oil

2 teaspoons freshly squeezed lemon juice

sea salt and freshly ground black pepper

SERVES 4–6

Put the butter in a small saucepan and cook over high heat until it is melted. Add the flour to the pan and stir quickly to form a thick paste. Remove from the heat and add a little of the milk, stirring constantly until thick and smooth. Return the pan to medium heat and add the remaining milk, whisking constantly until all the milk is incorporated and the mixture is smooth and thick. Add the cheese and stir until melted. Remove from the heat and let cool.

Preheat the oven to 220°C (425°F) Gas 7.

Remove the stalks from the mushrooms and sit the mushrooms in a small baking dish, gill side up. Spoon the cheese sauce into the caps and sprinkle the paprika over the top. Cook in the preheated oven for 20 minutes, until the mushrooms are soft and the sauce is golden and bubbling.

While the mushrooms are cooking, slice the fennel bulb as finely as possible, chop the fronds and put in a bowl with the parsley, oil and lemon juice. Toss to combine, season to taste and serve with the warm mushrooms.

spanish tortilla
tortilla española

Tortilla española is recognized as Spain's national dish. It's a favourite, eaten at all times of the day. Tapas bars frequently serve this tortilla cut up into bite-sized chunks. It can be made in advance and even tastes better that way.

100 ml/¼ cup olive or sunflower/safflower oil

4 potatoes, about 500 g/1 lb., cut into 1-cm/½-inch cubes

1 onion, thinly sliced

6 eggs

sea salt and freshly ground black pepper

a 24-cm/9 inches heavy non-stick frying pan/skillet (measure the base, not the top)

SERVES 4

Heat 2 tablespoons of the oil in the frying pan/skillet. Add the potatoes and cook over medium heat for 5 minutes. Add the onion and cook for 10 minutes or until the potatoes are almost tender, lifting and turning occasionally. Remove the potatoes and onions with a slotted spoon and drain on paper towels. Set aside the oil.

Put the eggs, salt and pepper in a bowl and beat with a fork. Add the potatoes and onions to the bowl, stir gently, then set aside for 10 minutes.

Put 2 tablespoons of the reserved oil in the frying pan/skillet and heat until smoking. Pour in the potato and egg mixture, spreading the potatoes evenly in the pan. Cook for 1 minute, then reduce the heat to medium and shake the pan often to stop it sticking. When the eggs are brown underneath and the top nearly firm, put a plate the same size as the pan on top and flip the tortilla onto it. Add 4 tablespoons of the remaining oil to the pan and slide the tortilla back into the pan. Cook for another 2–3 minutes until lightly browned on the other side.

Serve hot or at room temperature, cut into squares.

mushroom and pepper tortilla tapas

Any tortilla can be served as tapas; however, this recipe makes it even easier because it's cooked in the oven. If you want to make the tapas in advance, serve them cold or reheat for a few minutes in a medium oven. They are delicious served with a chilled fino or amontillado sherry.

3 tablespoons olive or sunflower/safflower oil

2 medium potatoes, about 250 g/ 8 oz., peeled and thinly sliced

1 small onion, halved and thinly sliced

75 g/3 oz. button mushrooms, sliced

1 orange bell pepper, halved, deseeded and cut into strips

5 large eggs

2 teaspoons chopped fresh oregano

sea salt and freshly ground black pepper

a 20-cm/8-inch shallow non-stick cake pan

a large heavy frying pan/skillet

SERVES 4

Preheat the oven to 200°C (400°F) Gas 6. Pour 1 tablespoon of the oil into the cake pan and put in the oven to heat.

Meanwhile, heat the remaining oil in the frying pan/skillet, add the sliced potatoes and onion and cook over medium heat for about 15 minutes, turning occasionally, until almost tender. Add the mushrooms and pepper and cook for 5 minutes.

Break the eggs into a large bowl and whisk briefly with a fork. Add the oregano and season with salt and pepper. Remove the vegetables from the pan with a slotted spoon, add to the bowl of eggs and stir gently.

Transfer to the preheated cake pan, return to the oven and cook for 15–20 minutes or until the egg is just set in the centre. Serve the tortilla hot or at room temperature, cut into small squares.

chickpea tortilla
tortilla de garbanzos

Although potato is the traditional ingredient in a Spanish omelette, chickpeas
are a delicious alternative, adding a slightly sweet, nutty flavour.

5 large eggs

$\frac{1}{2}$ teaspoon oak-smoked sweet
Spanish paprika

3 tablespoons chopped fresh
flat leaf parsley

3 tablespoons olive or
sunflower/safflower oil

1 large onion, finely chopped

I red bell pepper, halved, deseeded
and chopped

2 garlic cloves, finely chopped

400 g/2 cups canned chickpeas,
rinsed and well drained

sea salt and freshly ground
black pepper

*a 20-cm/8-inch heavy non-stick frying
pan/skillet (measure the base, not
the top)*

SERVES 2–3

Break the eggs into a large bowl, add some salt, pepper and
the paprika and whisk briefly with a fork. Stir in the parsley.

Heat 2 tablespoons of the oil in the frying pan/skillet. Add the
onion and red pepper and cook for about 5 minutes until
softened, turning frequently. Add the garlic and chickpeas and
cook for 2 minutes.

Transfer to the bowl of eggs and stir gently. Add the remaining
oil to the pan/skillet and return to the heat. Add the chickpea
mixture, spreading it evenly. Cook over medium-low heat until the
bottom is golden brown and the top almost set.

Put a plate the same size as the pan/skillet on top and flip the
tortilla onto it. Slide the tortilla back into the pan/skillet and cook
for another 2–3 minutes until lightly browned on the other side.
Serve hot or at room temperature, cut into squares or wedges.

paella tortilla

This tortilla studded with chicken, calasparra rice and seafood has all the flavours of a traditional paella. Why not serve it in chunks alongside the artichokes with Serrano ham (page 80), salt cod and tuna salad (page 64) and garlic prawns (page 68)?

3 tablespoons olive or sunflower/safflower oil

1 skinless chicken breast, about 175 g/6 oz., cut into strips

1 onion, chopped

1 garlic clove, chopped

1 red bell pepper, chopped

2 tomatoes, chopped

100 g/½ cup short-grain Spanish rice, such as calasparra

a pinch of saffron threads, soaked in 2 tablespoons hot water

250 ml chicken stock/broth

150 g/6 oz. cooked mixed seafood, such as prawns/shrimp, mussels and squid rings

6 eggs

3 tablespoons frozen peas, thawed

sea salt and freshly ground black pepper

a 24-cm/12-inch heavy non-stick frying pan/skilet (measure the base, not the top)

SERVES 4–6

Heat 2 tablespoons of the oil in the frying pan/skillet, add the chicken and fry until browned. Transfer to a plate.

Add the onion, garlic and red pepper and sauté for 5–6 minutes, stirring frequently, until softened.

Stir in the tomatoes, rice and saffron and its soaking water and pour in the stock/broth. Add the chicken and season with salt and plenty of pepper. Cover and cook over gentle heat for about 20 minutes or until the rice is almost tender, adding a little more stock/broth if necessary.

Stir in the mixed seafood and cook for 5 minutes or until the rice is just tender and all the liquid has been absorbed.

Break the eggs into a large bowl, add salt and pepper and whisk briefly with a fork. Stir in the paella mixture and the peas.

Wipe out the pan/skillet with paper towels. Heat the remaining oil in the pan/skilet over medium heat. Add the tortilla mixture and cook over medium-low heat for about 10 minutes until the bottom is golden brown and the top almost set.

Slide under a preheated grill/broiler to set and lightly brown the top. Serve hot or warm, cut into squares or wedges.

Note If ready-mixed seafood cocktail is unavailable, use 50 g/½ cup each of cooked peeled prawns/shrimp, shelled mussels and squid rings.

spinach and salt cod tortilla
tortilla de espinacas y bacalao

Salt cod with spinach makes a wonderful combination of flavours and textures. The addition of potatoes makes this tortilla quite hearty, so serve it alongside lighter dishes such as the Spanish roasted vegetables on page 96.

100 g/4 oz. boneless salt cod, cut into cubes

100 ml/¹/₂ cup olive or sunflower/safflower oil

250 g/8 oz. potatoes, peeled and thinly sliced

1 small onion, finely chopped

6 eggs

125 g/4 oz. cooked spinach, from 250 g/8 oz. uncooked

freshly ground black pepper

a 24-cm/8 inches heavy non-stick frying pan/skillet (measure the base, not the top)

SERVES 4

Prepare the salt cod as in the recipe on page 63. Alternatively, make your own salt cod (see note). Using your fingers, break it up into flakes.

Heat 80 ml/5 tablespoons of the oil in the frying pan/skillet, add the potatoes and cook over medium heat for 5 minutes. Add the onion and cook for 10 minutes or until the potatoes are almost tender, lifting and turning occasionally.

Lightly beat the eggs in a bowl with pepper. It usually isn't necessary to add salt because the fish is already salty. Mix in the spinach and flaked fish.

Pour the mixture into the pan/skillet, moving it with a spatula so that it flows under and over the potatoes. Cook until set on the bottom – shake the pan/skillet as it cooks and loosen the sides a little with a spatula. Put a plate on top of the pan/skillet, turn it upside down, then slide the tortilla onto the plate. Put the remaining oil in the pan/skillet. When hot, slide the tortilla back in, cooked side up. Cook for another 2–3 minutes until lightly browned on the other side. Serve hot or at room temperature, cut into squares or wedges.

Note To make your own salt cod, sprinkle a non-reactive dish with 75 g/3 tablespoons rock salt and put a 200 g/8 oz. skinless cod fillet on top. Cover with another 75 g/3 tablespoons salt and chill for 12 hours. Wash off the salt and soak in water for about 2 hours, changing the water several times.

tortilla with artichokes and serrano ham
tortilla de alcachofas y jamón serrano

Most tortillas are inverted onto a plate and returned to the pan to finish cooking. However, this tortilla is topped with Serrano ham and should be finished under the grill/broiler. You can trickle a little extra virgin olive oil over the top beforehand and, for a truly extravagant touch, add a few slices of goats' cheese log such as Soignon Petite Sainte-Maure, which melts beautifully into the top of the tortilla.

3 tablespoons olive or sunflower/safflower oil

3 medium potatoes, about 350 g/ 12 oz., peeled and cubed

1 Spanish onion, chopped

5 large eggs

400 g/2 cups canned artichoke hearts in water, well drained and halved

2 tablespoons fresh thyme leaves

100 g/3–4 oz. thinly sliced Serrano ham, torn into strips

6–8 slices of goats' cheese log with rind, about 125 g/4 oz. (optional)

sea salt and freshly ground black pepper

a 24-cm/12-inch heavy non-stick frying pan/skillet (measure the base, not the top)

SERVES 3–4

Heat 2 tablespoons of the oil in the frying pan/skillet. Add the potatoes and cook over medium heat for 5 minutes. Then add the onion and cook for a further 10 minutes, lifting and turning occasionally, until just tender. The potatoes and onion should not brown very much.

Meanwhile, break the eggs into a large bowl, season with salt and pepper and whisk briefly with a fork.

Add the artichokes, thyme and about three-quarters of the Serrano ham to the eggs. Next add the potatoes and onion and stir gently.

Heat the remaining oil in the frying pan/skillet. Add the tortilla mixture, spreading it evenly in the pan/skillet. Cook over medium-low heat for about 6 minutes, then top with the remaining ham. Cook for a further 4–5 minutes or until the bottom is golden brown and the top almost set.

Add the goats' cheese, if using, and slide under a preheated grill/broiler just to brown the top, about 2–3 minutes. Serve hot or warm, cut into wedges.

hearty country-style tortilla
tortilla campestre

A robust tortilla packed full of goodness, this is a perfect recipe for using up
small quantities of leftover vegetables, such as broccoli, corn, broad beans
or mushrooms. It is best to finish this tortilla under the grill/broiler to retain the lovely
colours on the top when serving, but you can also turn it over in the
pan/skillet to finish cooking it in the classic way.

4 tablespoons/$\frac{1}{4}$ cup olive or
sunflower/safflower oil

3 medium potatoes, about 325 g/
12 oz., peeled and cubed

1 onion, halved and sliced

75 g/about $\frac{1}{2}$ cup green beans,
trimmed and cut into thirds

4 asparagus spears, cut into 5-cm/
2-inch lengths

1 red bell pepper, quartered,
deseeded and thinly sliced

75 g/3 oz. cooked chorizo, sliced

1 garlic clove, finely chopped

6 large eggs

75 g/$\frac{1}{2}$ cup frozen peas, thawed

sea salt and freshly ground
black pepper

*a 24-cm/12-inch heavy non-stick
frying pan/skillet (measure the base,
not the top)*

SERVES 4–6

Heat 2 tablespoons of the oil in the frying pan/skillet. Add
the potatoes and cook over medium heat for 5 minutes.
Add the onion and cook for 10 minutes or until the potatoes
are almost tender, lifting and turning occasionally.

Meanwhile, put the beans and asparagus in a saucepan
of boiling, salted water and cook for 5 minutes. Drain and
refresh in cold water. Drain well.

Add the pepper, chorizo, asparagus, beans and garlic to
the potatoes and cook for 5 minutes, stirring frequently.

Break the eggs into a large bowl, add salt and pepper
and whisk briefly with a fork. Mix in the peas and cooked
vegetable mixture.

If necessary, wipe out the frying pan/skillet with paper towels,
then add the remaining oil and heat until hot. Add the tortilla
mix, letting it spread evenly in the pan.

Cook over medium-low heat for about 10 minutes until the
bottom is golden brown and the top almost set. Slide under
a preheated grill/broiler to set and lightly brown the top.
Serve hot or warm, cut into wedges.

UK sources

Brindisa
www.brindisa.com
Offers a fine selection of Spanish cheeses, hams and more.

Delicioso
www.delicioso.co.uk
Sells membrillo and other Spanish goods.

Fratelli Camisa
www.camisa.co.uk
This online delicatessen may be predominantly Italian but it's great for Spanish cured meats and a good selection of olive oils.

Seasoned Pioneers
www.seasonedpioneers.co.uk
Stocks a wide range of spices and seasonings, including smoked paprika and organic Spanish saffron.

Waitrose
www.waitrose.com
Manchego, membrillo, piquillo peppers and more.

US sources

Amigo Foods
www.amigofooods.com
A wide choice of foods from Spain including chorizo and Serrano ham.

Delicias de España
www.deliciasdeespana.com
Stocks a good range of Spanish foods and dishes.

The Spanish Table
www.spanishtable.com
For cazuelas, Serrano ham, Manchego and more.

La Tienda
www.tienda.com
Sells sweet smoked paprika, piquillo peppers, salt cod, chorizo cooking sausage, among other Spanish treats.

index

recipe credits

picture credits

KEY:
a=above, b=below, r=right, l=left,
c=centre.

Martin Brigdale
Pages 1, 4b, 5cr, 5br, 6, 8, 12, 13,
14, 15, 18, 22, 30, 32, 41, 42, 46,
49, 53, 54, 61, 65, 69, 72, 81, 86,
90, 93, 94, 97, 98, 101, 109, 110,
114, 120, 123, 124, 136

Peter Cassidy
Endpapers Pages 2, 4a, 5l, 5ar, 10,
17, 21, 25, 26, 28, 29, 34, 37, 38,
45, 47, 50, 52, 57, 62, 66, 70, 73,
77, 82, 85, 89, 99 inset, 102, 103,
105, 106, 113, 116, 119, 135, 144

Tara Fisher
Pages 117, 128, 131, 132, 139,
140

Richard Jung
Pages 9, 27, 75, 80, 107, 127

Kate Whitaker
Pages 23, 44, 58, 78, 99
background

Diana Miller
Page 40, 79

Noel Murphy
Pages 33, 74

David Brittain
Page 71

Nicki Dowey
Page 11

Gus Filgate
Page 76

Lisa Linder
Page 24

Debi Treloar
Page 115

Chris Tubbs
Page 3